HANDBOOK FOR TITLE MEN

Title Insurance and Trust Company's

Handbook

FOR

Title Men

Title Insurance and Trust Company

HOME OFFICE
LOS ANGELES : 1962

EIGHTH EDITION

ANDERSON, RITCHIE & SIMON : THE WARD RITCHIE PRESS

FOREWORD

THIS BOOK, now in its eighth edition, is a guide for the use of this Company's employees in meeting the title insurance requirements of the land-buying public.

In addition to its being used by our own employees, we believe it is helping to make uniform the practices of the title companies of California and that it is strengthening the understanding that exists between corporations insuring titles and individuals seeking title insurance.

There have been so many legislative changes since 1954, the date of the last revision, that the present edition is made necessary.

This HANDBOOK FOR TITLE MEN is a compilation originally made under the direction of W. W. Robinson when with this Company, and brought down to date by Arthur G. Bowman, Associate Counsel.

Where possible the system of paragraph numbering that was used in previous editions has been retained.

ERNEST J. LOEBBECKE

PRESIDENT

Title Insurance and Trust Company

Los Angeles, July, 1962

CONTENTS

HANDBOOK FOR TITLE MEN

ACCRETION

1.01   Accretion is the increase or acquisition of land by the gradual or imperceptible action of natural forces, as by the washing up of sand or soil from the sea or river, or by a gradual recession (called **reliction**) of the water from the usual watermark.

1.02   By accretion the added land (called **alluvion**) becomes the property of the owner of the land to which it is added.

1.03   Filled-in land is not land acquired by natural accretion and does not become the property of the owner of the adjoining land.

1.04   The **sudden** removal of land from the estate of one man to that of another by an inundation or by a **sudden** change in the course of a river is called **avulsion**. The owner of the part carried away may reclaim it within a year after the owner of the land to which it has been united takes possession thereof.

1.05   Before insuring the title to all lands bordering on salt or fresh water, a title company will investigate the character of such lands.

1.06   Where the channel of a **navigable river** has changed from causes other than accretion the title to the land within the dry bed of the original channel may be in the State of California. (A quiet title action against the State of California is permitted—under Section 6461 of the Public Resources Code—if the State claims title to property in a former bed of a navigable river.)

1.07   When a navigable river or slough is abandoned and no longer useful for navigation, the State Lands Commission may sell for cash to abutting property owners or anyone having an equitable interest—with a patent issued.

ACKNOWLEDGMENTS

2.01 **ACKNOWLEDGMENT DEFINED**

A formal declaration before a duly authorized officer by a person who has executed an instrument that such execution is his act and deed.

2.02 **REASON FOR**

To entitle an instrument (with certain specific exceptions) to be recorded, to impart constructive notice of its contents and to entitle the instrument to be used as evidence without further proof.

2.03 **EFFECT OF FAILURE TO ACKNOWLEDGE**

Unless by statute an acknowledgment is made essential to the validity of an instrument, such instrument is valid as between the parties and persons having actual notice of it even if not acknowledged. The time of acknowledgment is immaterial, if the rights of innocent third parties do not intervene.

2.04 **WHAT MAY BE ACKNOWLEDGED**

Every private writing, except last wills and testaments.

2.05 **CURATIVE ACT** (in effect July 29, 1927)

Cured all defects in acknowledgments (also the omission of acknowledgments) in all instruments recorded prior to July 29, 1926, and in all instruments thereafter that have been of record for one year (thus being an automatic Curative Act for the future). Section 1207, C.C.)

Except:

A—Instruments creating, abandoning, conveying, or encumbering marital homestead property must be acknowledged to be effective. (See Sections 1242 and 1243, C.C.)

B—Instruments executed by married women prior to March 14, 1895, since Section 1093 of the Civil Code, providing that no estate passed by her grant unless ac-

4

knowledged, was not amended until that date. See Section 2.11—under this topic.

BY WHOM ACKNOWLEDGMENTS MAY BE TAKEN:

2.06 **In This State:**

A—At any place within the state before a justice or clerk of the supreme court, a justice or clerk of any district court of appeal, a judge of a superior court, or a notary public (after September 17, 1959). Prior to the latter date a notary could not act outside the county for which he was appointed. (Section 1180, C.C.) Also specified officers of the United States armed forces. (See Sec. 2.09.)

B—Within the county or city and county in which the office was elected, or appointed, before either: a clerk of a municipal or justice court; a county recorder; a county clerk; a court commissioner; a district attorney; a judge of a municipal or justice court. (Section 1181, C.C.)

C—Before a deputy, if any of the officers mentioned in A and B, except officers of the armed forces, are authorized by law to appoint a deputy. (Section 1184, C.C.)

Section 1181 of the Civil Code was amended in 1959 to clarify the provision that the proof of acknowledgment of an instrument may be made before a notary public by specifying that it may be made before a notary public anywhere in the state. This made the Civil Code consistent with the provisions of the Government Code re notaries public. (Chapter 1970, Statutes of 1959)

2.07 **Without This State, But Within the United States:**

Within the jurisdiction of the officer, before either: a justice, judge or clerk of any court of record of the United States or of any state; a commissioner appointed by the governor of this state for that purpose; a notary public; or any other officer of the state where the acknowledgment is taken authorized by its laws to take such acknowledgment; or before a deputy if any of the officers herein mentioned are authorized by law to appoint a deputy. (Sections 1182, 1184, C.C.)

2.08 **Outside the United States:**

Before either: a minister, commissioner, chargé d'affaires, consul, vice-consul, or consular agent of the United States resident and accredited in the country where the acknowledgment is made; a judge of a court of record of said country; commissioners appointed for such purpose by the governor of the state pursuant to special statutes; a notary public; or certain officers of the United States armed forces; or before a deputy if any of the officers mentioned above are authorized by law to appoint a deputy. (Sections 1183, 1183.5, C.C.)

2.09 **By Officers of the United States Armed Forces:**

Certain commissioned officers of the United States armed forces may take acknowledgments of persons serving in or with the armed forces of the United States wherever located, as provided in Section 1183.5, Civil Code. Since September 11, 1959, the specified officers of the armed services may perform all notarial acts for spouses of members of the armed forces as well as for the members themselves. Any instrument acknowledged by any such officer or any oath or affirmation made before such officer is not rendered invalid by the failure to state therein the place of execution or acknowledgment. Authentication of the officer's certificate of acknowledgment is not required but the officer taking the acknowledgment must endorse or attach a certificate "substantially in a form authorized by the laws of this State" or in the form set forth in said Section 1183.5, C.C. (See Section 2.27 following.)

Commissioned officers given this power are:

1. Any officer of any component of the Army or Air Force of the United States on active duty in federal service commissioned in or assigned or detailed to duty with the Judge Advocate General's Department, any staff judge advocate or acting staff judge advocate, and

the adjutant, assistant adjutant, personnel adjutant or commanding officer of any command;

2. Any commanding officer or executive officer of a ship, shore station or establishment and any officer of or above the rank of lieutenant, senior grade, on active duty with the Navy or Coast Guard of the United States;

3. Any officer of or above the rank of captain on active duty with the United States Marine Corps.

2.10 Acknowledgments outside California— CERTIFICATE OF CONFORMITY

A certificate of acknowledgment executed outside of California by a notary or other authorized officer using the form authorized in California or the form authorized by the law of the place where the acknowledgment is made is sufficient in California. (Section 1189, C.C.)

If the form is proper, no certificate of conformity is necessary in order that the acknowledgment can be passed as sufficient for title insurance purposes.

If the form of the certificate of acknowledgment is not in accord with the law of California or that of the place where taken, it may be passed if there is attached the certificate of the clerk of a court of record of the county or district outside of California where the acknowledgment is taken to the effect that: (1) the officer certifying to the acknowledgment is authorized by law so to act; (2) the signature of said officer on the certificate of acknowledgment is true and genuine; and (3) the acknowledgment is taken in accordance with the laws of the place where made. (See Section 1189, C.C.)

2.11 BY MARRIED WOMEN

From January 1, 1873, to July 1, 1891, the certificate of acknowledgment of a married woman must set forth (in addition to the essentials of the general forms) that, upon an examination without the hearing of her husband, she was made acquainted with the contents of the instrument and thereupon acknowledged that she

7

executed the same and that she does not wish to retract such execution.

Prior to January 1, 1873, it was her acknowledgment only that must be separate and apart from and without the hearing of her husband, not including being "made acquainted with the contents of the instrument."

On July 1, 1891, the amendment abolishing the separate examination of a married woman took effect and on and after that date the general form of acknowledgment by the wife is sufficient. But a married woman's deed was required to be acknowledged up to March 14, 1895 and was invalid for all purposes unless acknowledged. Thus an acknowledgment by a married woman was imperative up to March 14, 1895, and the various curative acts did not cure the absence of such acknowledgment. On and after July 1, 1891, the general form was sufficient, but prior to that date the special form was necessary. On and after July 1, 1891, her signature and execution could be acknowledged by a subscribing witness.

2.12 VENUE

The venue (that is, the place where the acknowledgment was taken) must be stated to show that it was taken within the territorial jurisdiction of the officer.

By amendment of the Government Code in 1957 (Sections 8200 and 8205.1) it was required that notaries public shall reside or have their principal place of business in the county where appointed but may act as such notary in any part of the state. Accordingly, the rule was adopted that the county in which the acknowledgment is taken, as well as the county for which the notary's commission is issued, should be clearly indicated upon the document. This latter rule is no longer applicable, since the requirement that a notary public reside or have his principal place of business within the county for which he is commissioned to act was eliminated by statutory amendments in 1959.

2.13 MISTAKE IN DATE

A certificate of acknowledgment dated prior to the date of the instrument will be passed by a title company if it can determine that the discrepancy is obviously the result of clerical error.

2.14 AUTHENTICATION

The certificate must be authenticated by the signature of the officer, followed by the name of his office (or this may be stated in the body of the certificate or appear on his seal). His official seal must be affixed, if by law he is required to have a seal.

By amendment of Section 8205 of the Government Code in 1959, the name of the notary public must be typed or legibly printed under his signature on a certificate of acknowledgment.

2.15 SEAL OF NOTARY

Omission of seal, or defective seal, where the officer is required to have a seal, will not be passed by a title company. In this state, officers authorized to take acknowledgments, and required to have seals, are notaries and court commissioners. On a notary's seal must be engraved the State Seal, the words "Notary Public," and the name of the county in which he maintains his principal place of business. If he transfers his principal place of business to a different county than that shown on the seal, he must have the seal altered to indicate such change.

2.16 INTEREST OF OFFICER

An acknowledgment taken by a directly interested party, such as the grantee in a deed or the mortgagee in a mortgage, is void. An employee, or officer of a corporation, may take an acknowledgment, if not personally interested, and if he does not execute the instrument as an officer of the corporation, his duties as notary and as an officer of the corporation being distinct. Generally speaking, a husband or wife should not take the other's acknowledgment. If there are several parties to an instrument, whose interests are separate and distinct, an acknowledgment taken by one is valid as to the others, but not as to himself.

2.17 CORRECTION

An officer cannot amend or correct his certificate after delivery of the instrument. A new acknowledgment is necessary to entitle it to be recorded. An acknowledgment properly made, but defectively certified, may be corrected by a superior court action.

2.18 SIGNATURE BY MARK

The acknowledgment of a person who signs by mark may be taken in the usual form for acknowledgment of individuals, but two witnesses to the signature (of whom one may be the notary) are necessary to entitle the instrument to be acknowledged and recorded if executed subsequent to June 30, 1903. The name of the party signing by mark should be written near the mark by a person who writes his own name as a witness. (If there is but one witness and the instrument has been of record one year the Curative Act would appear to cure the defect since the requirement of **two** witnesses is to enable the instrument to be acknowledged.) (Also see Section 14.06.)

2.19 PROOF OF EXECUTION

Proof of the execution of an instrument, when not acknowledged, may be made by the party executing it; by a subscribing witness; or by other witnesses mentioned in the code section (1198, C.C.) providing for the proof of handwriting. (See Section 1195, C.C.)

2.20 RECORDING CERTAIN INSTRUMENTS PROHIBITED UNLESS ACKNOWLEDGED BY AFFECTED PARTY

There are certain instruments that cannot be recorded unless executed and acknowledged or proved by **the party who appears by the instrument to be the party whose real property is affected or alienated thereby.** These instruments, referred to in Section 27288, Gov. Code, are:

"An agreement for sale, lease, option agreement, deposit receipt, commission receipt, or affidavit which quotes or refers to an agreement for sale, lease, option agreement, deposit receipt, commission receipt or lease and such instrument claims to, or affects any interest in real property."

FORMS OF CERTIFICATES OF ACKNOWLEDGMENT

2.21 GENERAL FORM FOR INDIVIDUALS

STATE OF _____ $\Big\}$ ss.
COUNTY OF _____

On this _____ day of _____, in the year _____, before me (here insert the name and quality of officer), personally appeared _____ _____ known to me (or proved to me on the oath of _____) to be the person whose name is subscribed to the within instrument, and acknowledged that he (she or they) executed the same. (Section 1189, C.C.)

2.22 FORM FOR ATTORNEY-IN-FACT

STATE OF _____ $\Big\}$ ss.
COUNTY OF _____

On this _____ day of _____, in the year _____, before me (here insert the name and quality of officer), personally appeared _____ _____, known to me (or proved to me on the oath of _____·__) to be the person whose name is subscribed to the within instrument as the attorney-in-fact of _____, and acknowledged·to me that he subscribed the name of _____ thereto as principal and his own name as attorney-in-fact. (Section 1192, C.C.)

2.23 FORM FOR CORPORATION

STATE OF _____ $\Big\}$ ss.
COUNTY OF _____

On this _____ day of _____, in the year _____, before me (here insert the name and quality of officer), personally appeared _____ _____, known to me (or proved to me on the oath of _____) to be the president (or the secretary) of the corporation that executed the within instrument (where, however, the instrument is executed in behalf of the corporation by some one other than the president or secretary) insert: known to me (or proved to me on the oath of _____ _____) to be the person who executed the within instrument on behalf of the corporation therein named) and acknowledged to me that such corporation executed the same. (Section 1190, C.C.)

Note:

Section 1190.1, added to the Civil Code on September 22, 1951, provides:

"The certificate of acknowledgment of an instrument executed by a corporation, foreign or domestic, by its president or vice president and secretary or assistant secretary, other than an instrument conveying or otherwise transferring all, or substantially all, the assets of the corporation, may contain, in addition to the matters set forth in Section 1190 of this code, a statement substantially in the following form: 'and acknowledged to me that such corporation executed the within instrument pursuant to its by-laws or a resolution of its board of directors'; and such recital shall be prima facie evidence that such instrument is the act of the corporation, and that it was duly executed pursuant to authority duly given by its by-laws or the board of directors, and conclusive evidence of such matters in favor of any good faith purchaser, lessee or encumbrancer."

2.24 **FORM FOR CORPORATION ACTING AS ATTORNEY-IN-FACT** (Compiled)

STATE OF _____ ⎱
COUNTY OF _____ ⎰ ss.

On this _____ day of _____, in the year _____, before me (insert name and quality of officer), personally appeared _____, known to me to be the _____ President, and _____ _____ known to me to be the _____ Secretary of _____ and known to me to be the persons who executed the within instrument on behalf of said _____, the corporation that executed and whose name is subscribed to the within instrument as the attorney-in-fact of _____ and acknowledged to me that they subscribed the name of _____ thereto as principal and the name of _____ as attorney-in-fact for said _____, and that said _____ executed the same as such attorney-in-fact.

2.25 FORM FOR SUBSCRIBING WITNESS (Compiled)

STATE OF _____ }
COUNTY OF _____ } ss.

On this _____ day of _____, in the year _____, before me (here insert the name and quality of officer), personally appeared _____, known to me (or proved to me on the oath of _____ _____) to be the person whose name is subscribed to the within instrument as a witness thereto, who being by me duly sworn, deposed and said: that he _____ resides at _____; that he was present and saw _____ personally known to him to be the person described in and whose name is subscribed to the within and annexed instrument, execute the same; and that affiant subscribed his name thereto as a witness to said execution.

2.26 FORM FOR PARTNERSHIP

STATE OF _____ }
COUNTY OF _____ } ss.

On this _____ day of _____, in the year _____, before me (here insert the name and quality of the officer), personally appeared _____, known to me (or proved to me on oath of _____) to be one of the partners of the partnership that executed the within instrument, and acknowledged to me that such partnership executed the same. (Section 1190a, C.C.)

(This should be used in cases where the partnership as a legal entity is conveying or encumbering property.)

2.27 FORM FOR OFFICERS OF ARMED FORCES

The certificate of acknowledgment should be "substantially in a form authorized by the laws of this State or in the following form:

On this the _____ day of _____, 19____, before me, _____, the undersigned officer, personally appeared _____ known to me (or satisfactorily proven) to be serving in or with the armed forces of the United States (or to be the spouse of a member of the armed forces of the United States) and to be the person whose name is subscribed to the within instrument and acknowledged that ___he___ executed the same. And the undersigned does further certify that he is at the date of this certificate a commissioned officer of the rank stated below and is in the active service of the armed forces of the United States.

_____
_____

Signature of officer and serial number, rank, branch of service and capacity in which signed."

(Section 1183.5, C.C.)

2.28 FORM FOR CORPORATION AS A PARTNER OF A PARTNERSHIP

STATE OF _____ ⎱
COUNTY OF _____ ⎰ ss.

On this _____ day of _____, in the year ____, before me, _____, a Notary Public in and for said county and state, personally appeared _____, known to me to be the _____ President and _____, known to me to be the _____ Secretary of _____, the corporation that executed the within instrument and known to me to be the persons who executed the within instrument on behalf of said corporation, said corporation being known to me to be one of the partners of _____, the partnership that executed the within instrument, and acknowledged to me that such corporation executed the same as such partner and that such partnership executed the same.

AGREEMENTS OF SALE

3.01   The vendee (purchaser) under an agreement of sale has an **equitable** title in the property purchased. The vendor (seller) has the **legal** title. The interest of either may be conveyed or encumbered. However, under the provisions of C.C. Section 2985.1, added in 1961, a real property sales contract may not be transfered by the fee owner of the real property unless accompanied by a transfer of the real property which is the subject of the contract, and real property may not be transferred by the fee owner thereof unless accompanied by an assignment of the contract.

   The wife must join with the husband to convey his interest as vendee in real property.

3.02   **Money judgments** against the vendee are not a lien on his equitable title. The vendee's title, however, may be levied upon pursuant to a money judgment.

3.03   If the agreement is to be recorded, the **vendor must acknowledge** to impart constructive notice. Acknowledgment by the vendee alone is not sufficient to entitle the agreement to be recorded. (See Section 2.20.)

ALIEN LAND LAW

4.01   The Alien Land Law enacted in 1920, prohibited ownership of land by certain classes of aliens. This law was held unconstitutional on April 17, 1952 by the California Supreme Court in Sei Fujii v. State of California, 38 C.2d. 718, and in 1956 was repealed at the general election.

   Accordingly, all of the former rules of title practice based upon the restrictive provisions of the Alien Land Law are now disregarded by title companies. However, titles deraigned through escheat to the State under that law have presented problems requiring special consideration.

ASSESSMENTS
(See "Taxes and Assessments")

ATTACHMENTS
(Also see "Executions")

5.01 **DEFINITION**

An attachment is a seizure of defendant's property as security for any judgment plaintiff may recover in the action.

5.02 **PERIOD OF LIEN**

An attachment is a lien upon all real property attached for a period of 3 years after the date of levy, unless sooner released or discharged or unless the action be dismissed. (Sec. 542a C.C.P.)

After the expiration of 3 years from the recording of the attachment, it may be ignored unless:

1. An abstract of the judgment has been recorded; or

2. A levy of execution has been recorded; or

3. The attaching creditor or the defendant was in the military service at the end of the 3 year period or was in military service within 3 months immediately preceding the end of such period, in which case the period is extended until 3 months after the discharge of such party from military service; or

4. A certified copy of an order extending the attachment for not more than 2 years, obtained in accordance with the provision of Section 542a C.C.P., has been recorded prior to the end of the 3 year period.

5.03 **ATTACHMENT PRESERVES PRIORITY OF LIEN**

Even though the attachment lien has merged with the judgment lien, the judgment has priority over intervening liens—provided the attachment was *valid.*

(A title company cannot insure priority, however, since the attachment may be invalid for reasons not shown of record.) A purchaser at an execution sale acquires all interest of the judgment debtor on and after the levy of the attachment.

(A Federal tax lien, however, recorded after an attachment but before the recording of an abstract of judgment requires special consideration.)

5.04 **PRIORITY AS BETWEEN HOMESTEAD AND ATTACHMENT**

If a declaration of homestead is recorded before an abstract of judgment is recorded, a prior attachment, whether it is recorded before or after the homestead, must be shown in reports and policies despite the fact that, as a matter of law, the homestead may defeat the judgment lien.

There are three reasons for this rule. First, questions of fact which cannot be determined from the record might invalidate the homestead. Second, the attachment may have the effect of holding property so that if an execution is levied following the judgment, the creditor may be able to have the property sold to reach any excess over the statutory homestead exemption. (Sec. 1245 et seq. C.C.; Marelli v. Keating, 208 Cal. 528.) Third, the homestead property may be subject to execution or forced sale in satisfaction of judgments obtained for certain debts against which it does not provide exemption. (Section 1241, C.C.)

5.05 **DEED OR OTHER INSTRUMENT DATED PRIOR BUT RECORDED SUBSEQUENT TO ATTACHMENT**

Raises a question of fact as to the actual priority of the deed or other instrument in determining whether or not the attachment is a valid lien.

5.06 **ATTACHMENT MAY BE RELEASED OR DISCHARGED**

A—By the plaintiff, or his attorney, or by the officer who levied the writ (upon the plaintiff's instructions) by a writing signed, acknowledged and recorded. (Section 560, C.C.)

B—By the attaching officer, prior to making his return, on acceptance of an approved bond—in the manner provided by Section 540 C.C.P.

C—By a dismissal of the action.

D—By an order of court.

E—By the recording with the recorder of an abstract of the judgment in the action. (Section 542a, C.C.P.)

F—By the death of the defendant during the pendency of the action. (Myers v. Mott, 29 Cal. 359.)

5.07 **REAL PROPERTY HELD BY OR STANDING OF RECORD IN ANOTHER'S NAME**

Such property may be attached. The writ must describe said property, stating that the same and any interest of defendant therein, held by or standing in the name of such other person (naming him), are attached. A lien thereupon attaches to any interest defendant may have in the property, whether such interest appears of record or not.

5.08 **AFTER JUDGMENT HAS BEEN OBTAINED**

A—A valid attachment merges into a judgment lien. The attachment will not then be shown in a title policy, provided it is not "wild," though it will be shown in a preliminary title report. (As to when judgment becomes a lien, see Judgments, Section 31.02.)

B—If, however, there are liens intervening between a valid attachment and the judgment lien, the judgment is, by virtue of the attachment, prior to such intervening liens. A policy of title insurance, in such case, will show the judgment with a notation following that an attachment was levied on said property on a specified date, and the dates of recording the intervening liens will be shown in the write-up of such liens.

C—Prior to September 18, 1959, when the defendant recovered judgment against the plaintiff, plaintiff had 5 days after notice of entry of judgment within which to perfect an appeal and continue the attachment in force. Effective on the above date, Sections 553 and 946 C.C.P. were amended to provide for additional proceedings which result in a continuation of the attachment lien for longer period of time. Thus, the time within which an attachment remains in effect after judgment in favor of the defendant is extended if a motion for new trial is timely filed.

5.09 **ATTACHMENT OF PERSONAL PROPERTY**

An attachment or garnishment on personal property ceases to be of any force or effect three years after the issuance of the writ of attachment, if not sooner released or discharged. (Section 542b, C.C.P.) (This does not apply, however, to attachment of the interest of an heir, devisee or legatee in personal property belonging to the estate of a decedent.) (Section 561, C.C.P.)

BANKRUPTCY

6.01 **NATURE OF PROCEEDING**

A bankruptcy proceeding is one initiated under the federal statutes whereby an insolvent debtor may be adjudged bankrupt by the court, which thereupon takes possession of his property and distributes the proceeds proportionately among his creditors. A petition for adjudication may be filed by the debtor or by the requisite creditors.

6.02 **PURPOSE OF PROCEEDING**

A—To satisfy the claims of creditors.

B—To permit the bankrupt to acquire new property free of such claims to the extent allowed by the Bankruptcy Act.

6.03 **EFFECT OF ADJUDICATION**

An adjudication in bankruptcy brings the entire estate of the bankrupt owned by him at the date of filing the petition into the custody of the law.

6.04 **TITLE ACQUIRED BY TRUSTEE**

A—Upon appointment and qualification of a trustee, there is vested in him, **as of the date of the filing of**

the petition, the title to all non-exempt property owned by the bankrupt prior to filing the petition. (Section 70, Subd. a, of the Bankruptcy Act)

B—Property which becomes vested in the bankrupt **within six months after the filing of the petition in bankruptcy** by bequest, devise, or inheritance vests in the trustee (upon his appointment and qualification) as of the date when it vested in the bankrupt—free and discharged from any transfer made or suffered by the bankrupt after bankruptcy. (Section 70, Subd. a, of said Act)

6.05 **PROPERTY NOT SCHEDULED**

Property owned by the bankrupt at the time of filing the petition and not scheduled among the assets of the estate remains subject to the jurisdiction of the court, **if necessary to pay debts,** even after the discharge of the trustee; the proceedings may be reopened, if the claims are not fully paid, and a new trustee may be appointed to administer such property.

6.06 **EXEMPT PROPERTY**

Title to property exempt by the state law remains in the bankrupt, awaiting the legal formality of having it appraised and set apart to him. **Such an order should be obtained,** and thereafter the title to exempt property vests in him clear of the bankruptcy proceedings.

6.07 **BURDENSOME PROPERTY**

The trustee is not required to take title to burdensome property, such as unprofitable leaseholds or property subject to liens in excess of its value, and on an order being made releasing such property from the jurisdiction of the court it revests in the bankrupt.

6.08 **TRANSFERS MADE AND OBLIGATIONS INCURRED PRIOR TO BANKRUPTCY**

Every transfer made and every obligation incurred by a debtor who is or will thereby be rendered insolvent, *within four months* prior to the filing of a petition initiating a proceeding under the Bankruptcy

Act, is fraudulent as to present and future creditors: (a) if made or incurred in contemplation of the filing of a petition initiating a proceeding under said Act or in contemplation of liquidation of all or the greater portion of debtor's property, with intent to use the consideration obtained for such transfer or obligation to enable any creditor of such debtor to obtain a greater percentage of his debt than some other creditor of the same class, and (b) if the transferee or obligee of such transfer or obligation at the time of the transfer or obligation, knew or believed that the debtor intended to make use of such consideration. (Section 67, Subd. d-3 of said Act.)

Certain transfers made and obligations incurred by a debtor *within one year* prior to the filing of a petition initiating a proceeding under the Bankruptcy Act may be fraudulent as to creditors (existing and future) under the provisions of said Section 67, Subd. d-2, and may be avoided by the trustee in bankruptcy.

6.09 **TRANSFERS OF PROPERTY OTHER THAN REAL ESTATE PRIOR TO ADJUDICATION OR TO RECEIVER'S TAKING POSSESSION**

After the bankruptcy petition has been filed and either before adjudication or before a receiver takes possession of the property of the bankrupt, whichever first occurs, a transfer of property **other than real estate** made to a person acting in good faith and without notice is valid against the trustee if made for a present fair equivalent value. If the transfer is not made for a present fair equivalent value, the transferee is accorded a lien upon the property so transferred to the extent of the present consideration actually paid therefor. (Section 70, Subd. d, of said Act.)

6.10 **PREFERENCES DEFINED**

A preference is defined as a transfer of any of the property of a debtor to or for the benefit of a creditor for or on account of an antecedent debt, made or suffered by such debtor while insolvent and within 4 months before the filing by or against him of the petition initiating a proceeding under the Bankruptcy Act, the effect of which transfer will be to enable such creditor to obtain a greater percentage of his debt than some other creditor of the same class. (Section 60, Subd. a, of said Act.)

6.11 **LIENS ACQUIRED BY LEGAL PROCEEDINGS WITHIN THE FOUR-MONTH PERIOD PRIOR TO BANKRUPTCY**

Every lien against the property of a person obtained by attachment, judgment, levy, or other legal or equitable process or proceedings within four months before the filing of a petition initiating a proceeding under the Bankruptcy Act by or against such person shall be deemed null and void (a) if at the time when such lien was obtained such person was insolvent or (b) if such lien was sought and permitted in fraud of the provisions of the Act: **Provided, however,** That if such person is not finally adjudged a bankrupt in any proceeding under the Act and if no arrangement or plan is proposed and confirmed, such lien shall be deemed reinstated with the same effect as if it had not been nullified and voided. (Section 67-a (1) of the Bankruptcy Act.)

6.12 **FORECLOSURE OF LIENS AND DEEDS OF TRUST**

Where the power of sale under a deed of trust is to be exercised on property passing to a trustee in bankruptcy, it is necessary that leave of the bankruptcy court be first obtained to effect a valid sale.

6.13 **EFFECT OF BANKRUPTCY ON EXISTING LIENS**

Outstanding valid liens on the property of the bankrupt are not affected by bankruptcy proceedings, and title to the property passes to the trustee subject to such liens. The trustee, however, has the right to contest their validity by appropriate proceedings. Such contest may be made on the ground that the lien was fraudulently obtained, that it involved a preference, that it was obtained within four months of bankruptcy and void under Section 67 of the Bankruptcy Act; or the lien may be avoided on any other avoidable ground such as lack of consideration.

6.14 APPLICATION FOR DISCHARGE

The adjudication of any person, except a corporation, operates as an application for a discharge: Provided, That the bankrupt may, before the hearing on such application, waive by writing, filed with the court, his right to a discharge. A corporation may, within six months after its adjudication, file an application for a discharge in the court in which the proceedings are pending. (Section 14, Subd. a, of said Act.)

6.15 DEBTS NOT AFFECTED BY A DISCHARGE

A discharge in bankruptcy releases a bankrupt from all of his provable debts, whether allowable in full or in part, except such as:

(1) Are due as a tax levied by the United States, or any state, county, district, or municipality;

(2) Are liabilities for obtaining money or property by false pretenses or false representations or for obtaining money or property on credit or obtaining an extension or renewal of credit in reliance upon a materially false statement in writing respecting his financial condition made or published or caused to be made or published in any manner whatsoever with intent to deceive, or for willful and malicious injuries to the person or property of another, or for alimony due or to become due, or for maintenance or support of wife or child, or for seduction of an unmarried female, or for breach of promise of marriage accompanied by seduction, or for criminal conversation;

(3) Have not been duly scheduled in time for proof and allowance, with name of the creditor, if known to the bankrupt, unless such creditor had notice or actual knowledge of the proceedings in bankruptcy; or

(4) Were created by his fraud, embezzlement, misappropriation or defalcation while acting as an officer or in any fiduciary capacity; or

(5) Are for wages which have been earned within three months before the date of commencement of the proceedings in bankruptcy due to workmen, servants, clerks, or traveling or city salesmen, on salary or com-

mission basis, whole or part time, whether or not selling exclusively for the bankrupt; or

(6) Are due for moneys of an employee received or retained by his employer to secure the faithful performance by such employee of the terms of a contract of employment. (Section 17 of said Act.)

6.16 DEBTS COMING INTO EXISTENCE AFTER FILING THE PETITION IN BANKRUPTCY

Such debts are not released by a discharge (even though arising out of contracts existing before, if they did not constitute **provable debts** at that time.)

6.17 NOTICE IMPARTED BY THE RECORDING OF CERTIFIED COPIES OF ORDERS, ETC.

As provided by the Bankruptcy Act, a certified copy of any order or decree entered in a proceeding under the Act is evidence of the jurisdiction of the court, the regularity of the proceedings, the fact that the order or decree was made, and the contents thereof, and, if recorded, imparts the same notice that a deed or other instrument affecting property, if recorded, would impart. (Section 21-f.) A title company, however, will not assume the proceedings to be regular. It will examine them.

6.18 ORDER CANCELING A JUDGMENT

Section 675b, C.C.P. provides in effect as follows:

At any time after one year has elapsed since a bankrupt was discharged, he may apply to the court in which a judgment was rendered against him for an order directing the judgment to be canceled and discharged of record. If it appears upon the hearing that he has been discharged from the payment of that judgment, or the debt upon which such judgment was recovered, an order must be made directing said judgment to be canceled. Where the judgment was a lien on real property owned by the bankrupt prior to the time he was adjudged a bankrupt, and not subject to be discharged or released under the Bankruptcy Act, the lien upon said real estate shall not be affected by said order.

6.19 CORPORATE REORGANIZATIONS

Corporate reorganizations are provided for in Chapter X, Sections 101 to 276, both inclusive, of the Bankruptcy Act in effect September 22, 1938. This Chapter is a re-writing of old Section 77-B.

6.20 COMPOSITIONS AND EXTENSIONS IN CONNECTION WITH UNSECURED DEBTS

Chapter XI, entitled "Arrangements," comprising Sections 301 to 399, both inclusive, of the Bankruptcy Act, in effect September 22, 1938, supplants old Sections 12, 13, and 74 in so far as the relations between the debtor and **unsecured** creditors are concerned. Corporations and persons who could become bankrupt under Section 4 of the Bankruptcy Act, may avail themselves of the benefits of this chapter.

6.21 COMPOSITIONS AND EXTENSIONS IN CONNECTION WITH SECURED DEBTS, THE DEBTOR NOT BEING A CORPORATION

Chapter XII, entitled "Real Property Arrangements by Persons other than Corporations," comprising Sections 401 to 526, both inclusive, of the Bankruptcy Act in effect September 22, 1938, provides a system whereby persons other than corporations can make composition and extension settlements where secured, as well as unsecured, creditors are involved.

6.22 WAGE EARNERS' RELIEF

Chapter XIII, of said Act, in effect September 22, 1938, amended, entitled "Wage Earners' Plans," comprising Sections 601 to 686, both inclusive, provides for wage earners making settlement with their creditors out of future earnings by setting aside a part thereof by way of periodical payments extending over a protracted time. A wage earner is defined as meaning an individual whose principal income is derived from wages, salary or commissions. Prior to the 1959 amendment to chapter XIII, the relief was afforded to a wage earner whose annual income did not exceed $5000.00. The purpose of the 1959 amendment is to remove the monetary restriction and make it available to any insolvent debtor regardless of his total income.

6.23 **LOS ANGELES IN CENTRAL DIVISION OF SOUTHERN CALIFORNIA**

Since March 1, 1929 Los Angeles has been in the Central Division—and prior to that date in the Southern Division—of the Southern District of California.

BOND ISSUES BY CORPORATIONS OR INDIVIDUALS

7.01   Bond or note issues by **corporations or individuals** come under the jurisdiction of the state corporation commissioner **if the bonds or notes are to be offered to the public in California**—with certain exceptions. (See CORPORATE SECURITIES ACT, herein, Section 12.01 et seq.)

7.02   Before filing a trust deed or mortgage given to secure a bond or note issue that comes under such jurisdiction, a title company will require a copy of the state corporation commissioner's permit authorizing the issue.

7.03   A trust deed or mortgage executed by a **corporation** and given to secure a bond or note issue is required to have affixed thereto and canceled thereon **internal revenue stamps** in the proper amount. The rate is, on each $100.00 of face value or fraction thereof, eleven cents—of bonds actually being issued. (26 U.S.C.A. Sec. 4311) If there are later issues secured by the same trust deed or mortgage, additional stamps should be affixed by the trustee to the original trust deed or mortgage, but the same need not be recorded. (If the trust deed or mortgage is executed by an individual, no stamps are required.)

7.04   The county recorder should be directed as to the proper indexing (deed, trust deed, mortgage, chattel mortgage, bill of sale or power of attorney) when filing such trust deed or mortgage.

7.05   The only corporations that can act as trustees in bond issues are local national banks and domestic banks and trust companies.

BUILDING CONTRACTS
(Also see "Mechanics' Liens")

8.01   The filing in the office of the county recorder of the county wherein the land is situated, before the commencement of the work, of the original contract between the contractor and the owner is the equivalent of giving **actual notice** of the terms of the contract by the owner to all persons performing work or furnishing material thereunder. (Section 1185.1, C.C.P.)

8.02   The contract, though not so filed, is valid as to all persons, except that when not filed, liens, other than those of the contractor, are not limited by the contract price.

8.03   **FILING OF BUILDING CONTRACT NOT COMMENCEMENT OF WORK**

The filing of a building contract in the office of the county recorder does not constitute the commencement of work and does not affect the priority of a mortgage or deed of trust.

CHATTEL AND CROP MORTGAGES

9.01 **WHAT MAY BE MORTGAGED**

Mortgages may be made upon all growing crops, including grapes and fruit, and upon any and all kinds of personal property, except the following:

A—Personal property not capable of manual delivery;

B—Articles of wearing apparel and personal adornment;

C—The stock in trade of a merchant. (Sec. 2955, C.C.)

9.02 **FORM OF PERSONAL PROPERTY MORTGAGE**

A mortgage of personal property or crops shall be clearly entitled on the face thereof, apart from and preceding all other terms of the mortgage, to be a mortgage of crops and chattels, or either, and such mortgage may otherwise be made substantially in the form provided in Section 2956 C.C.

9.03 **WHEN VOID AS TO THIRD PARTIES** (as provided for in Section 2957, C.C.)

A mortgage of personal property or crops is void as against creditors of the mortgagor and subsequent purchasers and encumbrancers of the property in good faith and for value, unless:

A—It is acknowledged or proved and certified in like manner as grants of real property. (In mortgages executed prior to September 15, 1935, an affidavit of good faith also was required);

B—The mortgage, if of animate personal property other than crops growing or to be grown, is recorded in the office of the recorder of the county where the mortgagor resides at the time the mortgage is executed, or in case the mortgagor is a non-resident of this State, in the office of the recorder of the county where the property mortgaged is located at the time the mortgage is executed;

C—The mortgage, if of crops growing or to be grown, is recorded in the office of the recorder of the county where the land is located upon which such crops are growing or to be grown;

D—The mortgage, if of personal property other than crops growing or to be grown or animate personal property, is "recorded in the office of the recorder of each of the counties where the property mortgaged is located *and* where the mortgagor resides at the time the mortgage is executed, provided that in case the mortgagor is a nonresident of this State no recordation where the mortgagor resides is required, and in case the property mortgaged is thereafter removed to another county of this State, either the mortgage is recorded in that county or there is or has been filed a statement of recordation as prescribed in Section 2965."

E—Each such mortgage is clearly entitled on the face thereof, apart from and preceding all other terms of the mortgage, to be a mortgage of crops and chattels, or either;

F—Within four years from the last recording or re-recording thereof, it be recorded in its entirety or in lieu thereof there be recorded a certificate executed by the mortgagor or mortgagee, or the successor in interest of either thereof, and recorded in the office of the recorder of each county in which the mortgage has been recorded, which said certificate shall be in substantially the following form:

By this Certificate of Recordation that certain mortgage made by _____, mortgagor, to _____, mortgagee, and dated the _____ day of _____, in the year _____, and recorded in the office of the recorder of the county of _____ on the _____ day of _____ in the year _____, in book _____ of _____ at page _____ (set forth if available the date and place of each recordation), be and the same thereby is re-recorded.

(Signed) A.B.

(Mortgages made pursuant to court order, or securing bond issues authorized by the commissioner of corporations, or executed by a public utility need not be re-recorded to remain valid and effective as against creditors and subsequent purchasers and encumbrancers.)

9.04 FICTITIOUS MORTGAGES

A "fictitious mortgage" of personal property or crops may be recorded, if it has a notation upon its face that it is fictitious. Thereafter any of its provisions may be included by reference, without setting the same forth in detail, in any mortgage of personal property or crops recorded in the same county in which the fictitious mortgage is recorded. The fictitious mortgage need not be acknowledged or proved or certified to be entitled to record. (Section 2963, C.C.)

Section 2963 of the Civil Code was amended in 1961 to conform the provisions respecting the manner of making reference to recorded fictitious mortgages of personal property and crops to that applying to fictitious mortgages and deeds of trust on real property. The proper reference in either instance now is to the first page of the record of the fictitious mortgage or trust deed.

9.05 HOW FORECLOSED

The mortgagor's right of redemption may be foreclosed by a sale at public auction in the manner prescribed for "pledges" (see Section 2967, Civil Code) or by judicial sale under the direction of the court. Sales of personal property are absolute, the mortgagor having no right of redemption.

COMMUNITY AND SEPARATE REAL PROPERTY

10.01 DEFINITIONS

A—Community Property: Property acquired during marriage by either husband or wife, or both, that is not separate property.

B—Separate Property:
  (a) That acquired before marriage.
  (b) That acquired after marriage by gift, bequest, devise or descent, with the rents, issues and profits thereof. (It is not to be assumed that property distributed by a decree of distribution is separate property, where one or more of the heirs or devisees have assigned or deeded their interest to the distributee prior to the decree, since a valuable consideration may have been paid and **that portion of the property,** accordingly, may be community property.)
  (c) That conveyed by either husband or wife to the other with the intent of making it the latter's separate property.

(d) The earnings and accumulations of the wife, and of her minor children living with her, or in her custody, while she is living separate from her husband.

(e) The earnings and accumulations of each party after rendition of a judgment or decree of separate maintenance.

(f) Since 1959, the earnings and accumulations of the husband after an interlocutory decree of divorce and while the parties are living separate and apart.

(g) The earnings and profits of the wife from the conduct of a business as a sole trader.

(h) Damages awarded to either party in a civil action for personal injuries where the cause of action arises after September 11, 1957.

C—Quasi-Community Property: In 1961 the legislature amended the law to create a classification of "quasi-community property" which includes all personal property wherever situated and all real property situated in the State heretofore or hereafter acquired (a) by either spouse while domiciled elsewhere which would have been community property of the spouses had the spouse acquiring the property been domiciled here at its acquisition, or (b) in exchange for real or personal property, wherever situated, acquired other than by gift, devise, bequest or descent by either spouse during the marriage while domiciled elsewhere. Such property is treated similarly to that accorded community property with respect to dissolution of the marriage, homestead, taxation and the like.

10.01a PROPERTY CONVEYED TO A MARRIED MAN BY GIFT DEED

Property conveyed to a married man by a gift deed, except a deed from wife to husband as in 10.09, cannot be treated by a title company as his separate property so as to avoid the necessity of his wife joining in conveyances or encumbrances. The fact that the conveyance is in the form of a gift deed cannot conclusively establish the fact that the property is in fact a gift, and, therefore, the separate property of the husband.

10.02 PROPERTY ACQUIRED BY A MARRIED WOMAN PRIOR TO MAY 19, 1889

A—This is **presumptively community property** (unless it was acquired by gift, bequest, devise, descent, or by deed from her husband making it her separate property).

B—The husband must join in all deeds of such property, but failing to do so, he or his heirs or assigns will be barred from asserting any rights **after one year** from the date of recording the deed. The husband is a necessary party in actions involving the property.

C—Judgments against the husband are a lien on such property. The husband's name should be run by searchers for probate and other matters.

D—If the property acquired prior to May 19, 1889, in the wife's name is **actually** community property, the husband has complete control over it and can mortgage, or convey, without his wife joining in the mortgage or deed.

10.03 PROPERTY ACQUIRED BY A MARRIED WOMAN ON OR AFTER MAY 19, 1889

This is **presumed** to be her separate property. (It is her separate property, however, if acquired by gift, bequest, devise, descent, or by deed from her husband made with that intent.)

This presumption applies to **real property acquired on or after May 19, 1889,** and to **personal property acquired on or after July 29, 1927,** on which latter date Section 164 of the Civil Code was amended to include personal property.

This presumption is conclusive in favor of "any person dealing in good faith and for a valuable consideration with such married woman or her legal representatives or successors in interest, and regardless of any change in her marital status after acquisition of said property."

(See Section 10.07 for property acquired by **husband and wife on or after September 15, 1935.**)

10.04 PROPERTY ACQUIRED BY A MARRIED MAN PRIOR TO JUNE 1, 1891

This can be conveyed or encumbered by him without the wife joining in the instrument (unless a declaration of homestead has been recorded.)

10.05 COMMUNITY PROPERTY ACQUIRED BY A MARRIED MAN ON OR AFTER JUNE 1, 1891, AND PRIOR TO JULY 27, 1917

This cannot be conveyed by the husband without his wife's written consent (unless a valuable consideration is actually paid). The husband's conveyance without the wife joining in is insurable, however, one year after its recordation.

10.06 COMMUNITY PROPERTY ACQUIRED BY A MARRIED MAN ON OR AFTER JULY 27, 1917

A—Such property can be sold, conveyed or encumbered, or leased for a longer period than one year only by an instrument **jointly executed** by husband and wife —except that such an instrument by either spouse to the other is valid. (172a, C.C.)

The wife may join therein either personally or by her duly authorized agent. (172a, C.C.)

Should the wife not join with her husband, however, she has only **one year** after the recording of the instrument to commence an action to avoid the instrument. (172a, C.C.)

B—Any instrument executed **by the husband alone** is binding upon him, and in the hands of a purchaser, encumbrancer or lessee—in good faith, without knowledge or the marriage relation—is presumed to be valid. (172a, C.C.) Such an instrument, however, will not be insured by a title company until it has been of record one year.

C—The husband has the management and control of the community **real** property, subject to restrictions mentioned in A and B above. (172a, C.C.)

D—The husband has the management and control of the community **personal** property, with like absolute power of disposition, other than testamentary, as he has of his separate estate; provided, however, that he cannot make a gift of such community personal property, or dispose of the same without a valuable consideration, or sell, convey, or encumber the furniture, furnishings, or fittings of the home, or the clothing or wearing apparel of the wife or minor children that is community, without the written consent of the wife. (172, C.C.)

(See Section 10.07 for property acquired by husband and wife **on or after September 15, 1935.**)

10.07 PROPERTY ACQUIRED BY HUSBAND AND WIFE ON OR AFTER SEPTEMBER 15, 1935

This is presumed to be community property of the husband and wife, unless a different intention was expressed in the instrument by which they acquired, and provided the instrument described them as husband and wife. (164, C.C.) This presumption is not conclusive, and a title company will insist that each spouse join with the other in a conveyance or encumbrance.

In the case of the death of the wife, leaving no will, a title company will rarely rely upon the presumption that the property is community.

10.08 SUCCESSION TO COMMUNITY PROPERTY, THE RECORD TITLE BEING IN HUSBAND

A—Upon Death of Husband—

One half belongs to the wife; the other half is subject to the testamentary disposition of the husband and, in the absence thereof, goes to the wife. It is all subject, however, to the husband's debts and to administration of his estate.

B—Upon Death of Wife—

(a) **As to Property Acquired Prior to August 17, 1923:** The wife's interest was an expectancy only and died with her. A deed from the husband alone conveys good title, if the community is terminated by the wife's death either prior or subsequent to the deed.

(b) **As to Property Acquired Subsequent to August 17, 1923,** on which date the wife was given the right of testamentary disposition of one half of the community property. If the wife leaves no will the whole goes to the husband without administration. If she exercises her right to dispose of one half, that half is subject to administration. But after 40 days from the death of the wife, the surviving husband has power to convey, encumber, or otherwise deal with the property unless the claimants under the wife's will have recorded a notice that an interest in the property is claimed. Such notice must meet the requirements of Section 203, Prob. Code. A title company will require evidence that no will was left by the wife before insuring title in the husband alone or in the husband's grantees.

10.09 CONVEYANCE FROM ONE SPOUSE TO THE OTHER

When a husband or wife desires to convey to the other his or her community interest in property standing in the other's name, the deed executed should contain a recital that it is the grantor's intention to vest the title to the property described as the separate property of the grantee.

To convert property to community property, a deed executed by both husband and wife as grantors to themselves "as community property" is sufficient.

10.10 INSANE OR INCOMPETENT PERSONS, COMMUNITY PROPERTY OF

Where real property or any interest therein is owned by husband and wife as community property or where real property or any interest therein is owned as community or separate property and is subject to a homestead and one or both of the spouses is incompetent, it may be sold and conveyed or encumbered, transferred, or exchanged or otherwise disposed of either in the manner provided in Sections 1435.1 et seq., Prob. Code, or, since 1959, in guardianship or conservatorship proceedings with the consent of the sane spouse.

Under Prob. Code Sections 1435.1 et seq., the court may, in the proceeding provided for, judicially establish the fact of incompetency or insanity, the fact that the property is community, or the fact that a homestead is valid.

CORPORATIONS

FOREIGN CORPORATIONS
(Those organized outside the State of California)
Doing Intrastate Business in this State
(See Corp. Code, Sec. 6200 et seq.)

11.01 **OWNERSHIP OF REAL PROPERTY IN CALIFORNIA**

Any foreign corporation may acquire and hold real estate in California whether or not it be qualified to do business in this state. In order that any corporation can acquire and convey property in this state, it must, of course, have legal existence and must be in good standing in its home state as well as in this state at the date of any corporate act which is to be the basis of a title insurance policy.

Effective September 18, 1959, Corp. Code 6400 and 6401, which required the filing of articles of a foreign corporation with the Secretary of State and the County Clerk, were repealed. The filing of such articles is no longer required. In lieu of such filing, such a corporation must secure from the Secretary of State a certificate of qualification to do intrastate business in California. Failure to obtain such certificate subjects the delinquent corporation to a fine, and until it complies with the requirement, prohibits it from maintaining any action or proceeding in any court in this state upon any intrastate business so transacted.

Section 6600 of the Corporations Code was amended in 1961 to provide for the filing of incorporation papers of foreign corporations in the county clerk's office of any county in which such corporation held or holds real property.

11.02 **Taxes**

Foreign corporations doing an **intrastate business in this state** must pay the franchise tax levied by the State of California. Foreign corporations doing solely an interstate business are exempt from the franchise tax, but must pay a "corporation income tax" if they derive an income from sources within the state.

(For further information regarding taxes, see Section 11.06 et seq.)

11.03 **Forfeiture of right to do intrastate business** in the State of California results from failure of such foreign corporation to pay its franchise or income tax. (See topic—"Suspension," Section 11.08, and topic "Revivor and Restoration," Section 11.10.)

11.04 **TITLE COMPANY PRACTICE**

When title vested in or derived through a foreign corporation is to be insured, it must be determined that at the time of the acquisition or conveyance, or other corporate act upon the basis of which the policy is to be issued, the corporation was or is in existence and that its right to do business has not been revoked and was not and is not impaired by the failure to pay corporate taxes in that state. It must also be determined that the right of the corporation to do business in this state was not or is not supended by reason of its failure to pay California state franchise or corporate income taxes.

DOMESTIC CORPORATIONS
(Those organized within the State of California.)

11.05 **ARTICLES OF INCORPORATION**

A corporation is formed by the execution of articles of incorporation by three or more persons and the filing of the articles in the office of the secretary of state. A copy of these articles, certified by the secretary of state, and bearing the indorsement of the date of filing in his office, is then filed with the county clerk of the county in which the corporation has its principal office.

Since August 14, 1929, the corporate existence begins upon this filing of articles with the secretary of state and continues perpetually unless otherwise expressly provided by law.

There is also a requirement that a copy of the articles, certified by the secretary of state, shall be filed with the county clerk of every county in the state in which the corporation holds real property. The only penalty, however, for failure to do this is that the corporation cannot maintain an action or proceeding in relation to such real property.

Prior to July 29, 1921, a corporation's articles were filed first in the office of the county clerk, after which a copy certified by him was filed with the secretary of state.

TAXES AGAINST CORPORATIONS

11.06   Among the special taxes levied by the State of California, and to which corporations may be subject, are those enumerated and described as follows:

A—Bank and Corporation Franchise Tax:

A tax, based on net income for the next preceding income year, against banks, financial corporations, and general corporations—as specified in Chapter 2 of the Bank and Corporation Tax Law—and with a $25 minimum. (See Sections 23101 et seq., Revenue and Taxation Code.)

The first franchise tax act was effective April 1, 1911, and the taxes thereunder were a lien on real property. Prior to the fiscal year 1917-18, forfeiture of charter instead of suspension resulted from nonpayment.

B—Corporation Income Tax:

A tax upon the net income of every corporation deriving an income from sources within this State on or after January 1, 1937, other than income for any pe-

riod for which the taxpayer is subject to taxation under Chapter 2 of the Bank and Corporation Tax Law—
as specified in Chapter 3 of the Bank and Corporation
Code. (See Sections 23501 et seq., Revenue and Taxation Code.)

C—Motor Vehicle Fuel License Tax:

A tax against distributors of gasoline, including those
who refine, manufacture, produce, compound and sell
motor vehicle fuel in California.

D—Motor Vehicle Transportation License Tax:

A license tax upon individuals, firms, partnerships
and corporations engaged in the transportation on
public highways of persons or property for hire by
motor vehicles other than those operating exclusively
within incorporated cities or towns.

E—Private Car Tax:

A tax against the owners of private cars operated
upon railroads in the state (but not including freight
and passenger cars owned by railroad companies.)

F—Sales and Use Tax:

A tax for the privilege of selling tangible personal
property at retail imposed on all retailers and on the
storage, use, or other consumption in California of
such property purchased from any retailer.

11.07   Lien of Taxes Listed Above

By legislation effective September 19, 1947, the "se-
cret" lien provisions of the various laws imposing these
taxes were abolished. Thereafter any unpaid tax becomes a lien only upon the filing for record with the
county recorder of an abstract of judgment or a certificate specifying the amount, interest and penalty
due, the name and last known address of the person
liable, and the fact that compliance has been made with
the provisions for determination of the amount to be
paid. The lien continues for 10 years thereafter unless
sooner released or discharged. The lien may be extended within 10 years from the date of filing the abstract or certificate or within 10 years from the date of

the last extension by filing for record a new abstract or certificate with the county recorder. The effect of the extension is to extend the lien for 10 years unless sooner released or discharged. As to certain taxes, however, the lien may be extended for 5 years instead of 10.

The lien of these taxes may be **subordinated**, as provided for in each of the laws.

11.08 **Suspension**

Nonpayment of the **bank and corporation franchise tax** ultimately results in suspension of the corporate powers, rights and privileges of a domestic taxpayer and in the forfeiture of the exercise of the corporate powers, rights and privileges of a foreign taxpayer in this state. The certificate of the Secretary of State is prima facie evidence of such suspension or forfeiture. Every contract made in violation of the provisions relating to suspension or forfeiture is voidable at the instance of any party other than the taxpayer.

Nonpayment of the **corporation income tax** ultimately results in suspension of the corporate powers, rights and privileges of a domestic taxpayer in this state. The certificate of the Franchise Tax Board setting forth that the suspended taxpayer has been notified of its liability for tax and that such tax has not been paid is prima facie evidence of such facts.

11.09 **Forfeiture of the Charter**

The non-payment of a **license tax** (which tax was abolished by the 1927 Legislature) prior to the license tax for the year 1918 or the non-payment of a **franchise tax** prior to the franchise tax for the fiscal year 1917-18 resulted in **forfeiture** of the charter of domestic corporations. In other words, the corporation died, and its property became vested in the stockholders subject to the powers of the directors as trustees for the creditors and stockholders.

A deed out from such a defunct corporation should be executed by all of the directors as trustees and should contain full and proper recitals as to the forfeiture, the necessity of disposing of the property, the full consideration, and the statement that the grantors are **all** of the directors, and should be made, probably, pursuant to court order.

11.10 **Revivor and Restoration**

(Bank and Corporation Franchise Tax): Upon application to the Franchise Tax Board in writing and upon payment of taxes, deficiencies, interest and penalties, the Board issues a **certificate of revivor.** This certificate is prima facie evidence of the corporation's reinstatement "and such certificate may be recorded in the office of the county recorder of any county of this State."

(Corporation Income Tax)· Suspension is terminated on payment of the tax, and the certificate of the Franchise Tax Board that the tax has been paid is evidence of the termination of the suspension.

11.11 **EXECUTION OF INSTRUMENTS BY CORPORATION**

The name of the corporation should appear in the signature.

The **authorized** officers must sign on behalf of the corporation; usually they are the president or vice-president and secretary or assistant secretary. See Section 2.23, however, for recital in a corporation's acknowledgment that is prima facie evidence that instrument is act of corporation.

The corporate seal must be affixed, unless the officers have been specially authorized to execute without the seal. (The seal is prima facie evidence of the authority of the officer or officers to execute on behalf of the corporation, though it is not **conclusive** evidence.) The seal must show "the name of the corporation, and the state and date of incorporation." It must be "engraved, lithographed, printed, stamped, impressed upon or affixed to the instrument."

The acknowledgment must be according to the special form for corporations. (See Acknowledgments, Sections 2.23, 2.24.)

For conveyance by corporation after change of name, see Section 42.01.

11.11a SALE, MORTGAGE OF ENTIRE OR SUBSTANTIAL POR-TION OF ASSETS

A corporation may not sell, convey, lease, exchange or otherwise dispose of all or substantially all of its assets except on the authority of a resolution of its board of directors, and with the approval of the principal terms of the transaction and the nature and the amount of consideration by vote or written consent of shareholders entitled to exercise a majority of voting power, or a larger proportion of shareholders if the articles so require.

A certificate of the secretary or an assistant secretary of the corporation, however, may be attached to a deed or other instrument conveying or otherwise transferring property of the corporation, which certificate may either (1) set forth the resolution of the board of directors authorizing the conveyance or transfer of all, or substantially all, of the assets of the corporation, and stating the fact of approval thereof by the shareholders; or (2) state that the transfer is one of less than substantially all of the assets. Such a certificate is conclusive as to the facts therein in favor of an innocent purchaser for value.

RELIGIOUS, CHARITABLE, SOCIAL, EDUCATIONAL, RECREATIONAL AND CEMETERY CORPORATIONS

11.12   Section 9200 of the Corporations Code, in effect September 19, 1947, provides: "A nonprofit corporation may be formed by three or more persons for any lawful purposes which do not contemplate the distribution of gains, profits or dividends to the members thereof, and for which individuals may associate themselves, such as **religious, charitable, social, educational, recreational, or cemetery purposes, or for rendering services,** subject to laws and regulations applicable to particular classes of nonprofit corporations or lines of activity. Carrying on of business at a profit incidental to the main purposes of the corporation and the distribution of assets to members on dissolution are not forbidden to nonprofit corporations."

When passing upon an instrument, executed by a nonprofit corporation, a title company ordinarily will call for its by-laws to see that the proper officers have executed it and to see what restrictions have been placed upon their acts. For example, if the corporation is a church, the by-laws or constitution will show whether or not the congregation must approve the transaction in question or whether or not the consent of certain officials (treasurer, presiding elder, etc.) must be obtained. Resolutions will be called for showing that all requirements have been met and that the particular deed, mortgage or other instrument is authorized.

11.13   Prior to July 29, 1927, **religious, social and benevolent corporations** were required to obtain an order of court in order to convey, lease or encumber property, unless organized as nonprofit cooperative corporations.

11.14   Prior to August 14, 1931, **cemetery corporations** were required to obtain an order of court to sell real property, unless organized as ordinary corporations for profit. On that date the General Cemetery Act went into effect, governing the acts of cemetery corporations. Cemetery corporations have the same powers granted by law to corporations in general, including the right to borrow money and to secure the same by mortgage or deed of trust. Any such mortgage, deed of trust or other lien upon property dedicated as a cemetery (and any sales upon foreclosure) shall be subject and subordinate to such dedication. The statutory law pertaining to cemeteries is contained in the Health and Safety Code beginning with Section 7000.

11.15   **CORPORATION SOLE**

A **corporation sole** may be formed by the bishop, chief priest, presiding elder or other presiding officer of any religious denomination, society or church for the purpose of administering and managing the affairs, properties and temporalities thereof. It must file articles of incorporation. It has continuity of existence, notwithstanding vacancies in incumbency. It may sell, convey, lease, mortgage or otherwise deal in real and personal property in the same manner that a natural person may without an order of court. (Sections 10000 to 10015, Corporations Code.)

11.16 PUBLIC UTILITY CORPORATIONS

Public utilities are required to secure permission from the Public Utilities Commission, formerly Railroad Commission, before they may sell, lease, assign, mortgage, or otherwise dispose of or encumber property necessary or useful in the performance of their duties to the public.

Title companies, when called upon to pass upon a conveyance from a public utility corporation, will ask for evidence as to the use to which the property has been put or for the permit of the Commission.

11.16a MUTUAL WATER COMPANIES

A mutual water company which delivers water solely to its stockholders is not a public utility and, generally speaking, it has the same power to sell and encumber its properties as other private corporations. Any conveyance and encumbrance is subject, however, to certain rights in the property which nonconsenting stockholders may have.

If a mutual water company does deliver water to others than its members for compensation, it may become a public utility and be subject to the jurisdiction of the Public Utilities Commission.

11.17 WHEN CORPORATION DEEDS TO ONE OF ITS OFFICERS

A deed from a corporation by its officers to one of those officers will not be passed by a title company without the submission of a special resolution of the board of directors as evidence of the authority for the deed's execution.

DISSOLUTION OF CORPORATIONS

11.18 Since August 14, 1929, a corporation, whether it expires by its own limitation, by forfeiture of existence by order of court or otherwise, continues to exist for the purpose of winding up its affairs, prosecuting and defending actions by or against it, collecting and discharging obligations, disposing of and conveying property and collecting and dividing assets, but not for the purpose of continuing business except in so far as necessary for the winding up thereof.

(As to a corporation that dissolved prior to August 14, 1929, its assets could be sold, at least after July 27, 1917, only under court direction, the directors or managers of the corporation at the time of its dissolution, or other persons appointed by the court, executing the conveyance, they being the trustees of the creditors and stockholders.)

11.19   **Voluntary** winding up and dissolution is provided for in Part 9 of the Corporations Code.

A certificate giving **notice of the corporation's election** to wind up and dissolve (after proper authorization from the stockholders or, in special cases, by resolution of the directors) is filed in the office of the secretary of state and a copy, certified by him, in the office of the county clerk of the county in which the principal office of the corporation is located. The board of directors continues to act as a board and has full powers to sell, convey or otherwise dispose of any or all the assets and in general to make contracts and to do any and all things in the name of the corporation which may be proper or convenient for the purposes of winding up, settling and liquidating the affairs of the corporation.

When the corporation has been completely wound up without court proceedings, a certificate, signed by a majority of the directors or trustees, stating that the corporation has been completely wound up, its known debts and liabilities paid or provided for, its known assets distributed and its franchise tax paid, is filed in the office of the secretary of state and a copy, certified by him, in the office of the county clerk of the county in which the principal office of the corporation is located. Thereupon corporate existence ceases except for the purpose of further winding up, if needed.

(When called upon to pass a deed executed by a corporation that has voluntarily dissolved under said provisions of the Corporations Code, a title company will require that it be executed in the name of the corporation, by the executive officers, supported by a resolution of the board of directors specifically authorizing the deed and disclosing that it is in connection with the winding up of the corporation's affairs.)

UNINCORPORATED BENEVOLENT OR FRATERNAL SOCIETIES OR ASSOCIATIONS AND UNINCORPORATED LABOR ORGANIZATIONS

(See Sections 59.01, 59.02)

CORPORATE SECURITIES ACT
(BLUE SKY LAW)

12.01 **IN GENERAL:** The Corporate Securities Act (codified and comprising Sections 25000 to 26104 of the Corporations Code) provides that no company shall sell or offer for sale any **security** of its own issue until it has secured a permit from the commissioner of corporations.

The word "company" includes all domestic and private corporations, associations, joint stock companies, partnerships, and also trustees and individuals as defined in the act.

12.02 **DEFINITION OF SECURITY:** The word "security" includes any stock, bond, note, treasury stock, debenture, evidence of indebtedness, certificate of interest or participation, certificate of interest in a profit-sharing agreement, certificate of interest in an oil, gas or mining title or lease, collateral trust certificate, any transferable share, investment contract, or beneficial interest in title to property, profits or earnings, guarantee of a security and any certificate of deposit for a security.

(By reason of the broad definition of "security," a title company may question assignments of fractional

46

interests in oil or mining leases, deeds or assignments conveying a series of undivided interests in oil or oil land or deeds conveying a series of oil-bearing lots, or small portions of a lot or lots covered by a community oil lease, unless a permit covering such conveyances has been obtained from the corporation commissioner.)

12.03 **SECURITIES EXEMPT:** Except as otherwise expressly provided in the Corporate Securities Law, the following classes of securities, **among others,** are excepted from the provisions of the act:

Securities issued or guaranteed by the United States or by any state, county or municipality; securities issued by and representing an interest in or a direct obligation of national banks, companies organized under any act of congress, state banks, trust companies or savings institutions incorporated under the laws of this state; securities authorized by the Public Utilities Commission or Interstate Commerce Commission or by the Federal Power Commission; securities issued by companies subject to the supervision of the building and loan commissioner or insurance commissioner; any security **(except notes, bonds, debentures or other evidence of indebtedness)** issued by a company organized under the laws of this state exclusively for educational, benevolent, fraternal, charitable or reformatory purposes and not for pecuniary profit; any security which has been certified as a legal investment for savings banks and trust companies under the laws of this state; any certificate of deposit for any security which has been approved by the California District Securities Commission for certification as a legal investment for savings banks and trust companies under the laws of this state; bills of exchange, trade acceptances, promissory notes and other commercial paper issued, given or acquired in a bona fide way in the ordinary course of legitimate business, trade or commerce; promissory notes, whether secured or not, where the notes are not offered to the public, or are not sold to an underwriter for the purpose of resale; securities sold by a bona fide owner (not the issuer or underwriter) who sells the same for his own account and not for the purpose of evading the provisions of the act.) (See Sections 25100 et seq., Corporations Code.)

12.04 **INDIVIDUALS:** The act further provides that the word "individual" in so far as it is included in the definition of a "company" includes only persons selling, offering for sale, negotiating for sale, or taking subscriptions for any security of their own issue.

12.05 **STATUTE OF LIMITATIONS:** Section 336a, added to the Code of Civil Procedure on September 15, 1935, provides a period of **six** years within which an action may be commenced upon any bonds, notes or debentures issued by any corporation or pursuant to permit of the commissioner of corporations, or upon any coupons issued with such bonds, notes or debentures, if such bonds, notes or debentures shall have been issued to or held by the public; or upon any mortgage, trust deed or other agreement pursuant to which such bonds, notes or debentures were issued. (Section 336a does not "apply to bonds or other evidences of indebtedness of a public district or corporation.")

COVENANTS, CONDITIONS AND RESTRICTIONS

(For Covenants implied by grant, see "Deeds";
also see "Zoning")

13.01 **DEFINITION**

A covenant is an agreement, used generally in connection with instruments pertaining to real property, to do or not to do certain things, while a condition is a qualification annexed to an estate, upon the happening of which the estate is enlarged or defeated.

13.02 **DIFFERENCE**

Covenants and conditions differ in two respects: First, in regard to the relief awarded; and Second, as to the persons by or against whom they may be enforced.

13.03 **RELIEF AWARDED**

While a condition affects the estate created, and a failure to comply with it may result in a forfeiture of title, the only remedy for a breach of covenant is an action for damages or an injunction.

13.04 **WHETHER COVENANT OR CONDITION**

Since the law abhors forfeitures, the courts will construe the provisions as covenants only, unless the intent to create a condition is plain.

The use of the term "condition" or "covenant" is not always controlling. The real test is whether the intention is clearly expressed that the enjoyment of the estate conveyed was intended to depend upon the performance of the condition, otherwise it will be construed as a covenant only.

A deed reciting that it is given upon the agreement of the grantee to do or not to do certain things implies a covenant and not a condition. So also a recital that the land conveyed is or is not to be used for certain purposes; as "to be used for church purposes" or "that a school house be erected thereon."

13.05 **RE-ENTRY OR FORFEITURE CLAUSE**

Such a clause is not necessary to create a condition, although it is the better practice, since then the intention is plain.

The mere use of the word "condition" in a restriction may result in a forfeiture or reversion of title if a violation occurs, and in such instances if there is no **express** provision for forfeiture the deed is said to contain an **implied** reversion.

13.06 **CONDITIONS PRECEDENT AND SUBSEQUENT**

The former must be performed before the title will pass from the grantor, while a failure to perform the latter may result in a forfeiture of the title that has vested in the grantee.

13.07 **COVENANTS AND CONDITIONS THAT ARE ILLEGAL**

Covenants and conditions that are unlawful, impossible of performance or in restraint of alienation are void; otherwise a grantor may impose any conditions in a grant that he sees fit. Thus he may reserve the right to revoke the deed or sell the property, provided such reservation is not repugnant to the grant. (167 Cal. 570.)

A condition that a party shall not marry is void, but a condition to give use only until marriage is valid. A condition against conveying without the consent of the grantor, or only for a specified price, is void as in restraint of alienation. The title passes freed of a condition subsequent that is void. Title does not pass at all if a condition precedent is impossible of fulfillment or requires the performance of an act wrong of itself, but if the act be not wrong of itself, but otherwise unlawful, the deed takes effect and the condition is void. (A title company ordinarily will not insure that a particular condition is or is not void.)

13.08 **RACE RESTRICTIONS**

On May 3, 1948 the United States Supreme Court held that racial restrictive covenants could not be enforced in equity against Negro purchasers because such enforcement would constitute state action denying equal protection of the laws to Negroes, in violation of the Fourteenth Amendment to the Federal Constitution. (Shelley v. Kraemer, McGhee et ux v. Sipes et al.)

On May 18, 1948 the California Supreme Court referred to this decision and reversed the decisions of the several trial courts in the cases then before it which had undertaken to enforce such restrictive covenants. (Cummings et al v. Hokr et al.)

On and after February 15, 1950 the insurance by the Federal Housing Administration or by the Veterans Administration of loans secured by mortgages or trust deeds was made subject to regulations designed to discourage the practice of restricting real property against sale or occupancy on the ground of race, color, or creed.

On June 15, 1953 the United States Supreme Court

held that a restrictive covenant could not be enforced at law by a suit for damages against a co-covenanter who broke the covenant. (Barrows v. Jackson)

Since May 18, 1948 title companies, accordingly, have issued special insurance and lenders' policies insuring against loss by reason of violation of such covenants, but since the covenants were recognized as valid in and of themselves have hesitated to insure an owner against the existence of any such covenant.

(Under the rule as it existed in California before May 18, 1948, a provision in a deed against **sale, lease,** or **rental** of property to persons of an indicated race was regarded as a restraint on alienation, and, therefore, invalid. On the other hand, a restriction on the **use** or **occupancy** of property by persons or an indicated race was recognized as valid.)

In 1961 the California legislature added Section 782 to the Civil Code to provide that any provision in any deed of real property in California, whether executed before or after the effective date of the section, which purports to restrict the right of any person to sell, lease, rent, use or occupy the property to persons of a particular racial or ethnic group by providing for payment of a penalty, forfeiture, reverter, or otherwise, is void. See also Section 53 of the Civil Code.

If race restrictions are contained in instruments recorded prior to Feb. 15, 1950, they will be omitted in any evidence of title; those contained in instruments recorded on or after said date will be shown in evidence of title.

13.09 BUILDING AND LIQUOR RESTRICTIONS

Such may be imposed either as covenants or as conditions.

13.10 ELIMINATION OF RESTRICTIONS

Unless the language used in the deed creating the restrictions indicates definitely that the grantor intended the conditions or restrictions to operate for the benefit of other lots or persons, the restrictions run to the grantor only, and a quitclaim deed from him, or his heirs or assigns, is sufficient to release the restrictions.

If the language used in such deed shows, however, that the conditions or restrictions were intended for the benefit of adjoining owners or other lots, or owners in the tract, then quitclaim deeds must be obtained from all owners of lots having the benefit thereof, as well as from the grantor, or his heirs or assigns, in order to release the restrictions.

13.11 GENERAL PLAN OR SCHEME

If the record discloses that the conditions or restrictions are part of a general plan or scheme for the improvement of the entire tract, the conditions or restrictions will be shown in a policy of title insurance as affecting each lot in the tract, regardless of whether it has been deeded out or not, or of whether the deed of the particular lot omits them altogether.

DEDICATION GUARANTEE

(See Subdivision Guarantee, Section 34.02)

DEEDS

14.01 ESSENTIALS

A—Any form of written instrument, otherwise sufficient, which contains apt words of conveyance such as "grant," "transfer," or "convey" is sufficient to pass title to land. There is no fixed and absolute form. But it must contain the names of the grantor and grantee, and a description of the property conveyed sufficient for identification. A **seal** is not necessary.

B—The statutory or short form of grant deed is as follows:
"I, A. B., grant to C. D. all that real property situate (insert description).

Witness my hand this ＿＿＿＿＿＿ day of ＿＿＿＿＿＿, 19＿＿."

C—A **consideration** is presumed. It need not be stated in the deed. (In the case, however, of deeds made by administrators, executors, guardians, trustees, receivers, etc., who are conveying property under court order, the receipt of the exact amount should be recited.)

D—The absence of a **date** does not invalidate a deed.

E—**Delivery** is esential, delivery meaning "intent to deliver" and not necessarily physical delivery. A grant, to be effective, cannot be delivered to the grantee conditionally. A deed is presumed to be delivered at its date.

14.02 GRANT DEED—AND WHAT IT IMPLIES

The word **"grant"** when used in any conveyance of an estate of inheritance or fee-simple, unless restrained by express terms, implies, on the part of the grantor, for himself and his heirs, to the grantee, his heirs and assigns, that the grantor has not already conveyed to any other person; and that the estate conveyed is free from encumbrances made or suffered by the grantor, or any person claiming under him, including taxes, assessments and all liens.

This includes rights of way and building restrictions, but, otherwise, there is no implied covenant of warranty on the part of the grantor that he is the owner of the property.

A grant deed conveys the fee title, and any after acquired title of the grantor, unless a different intent is expressed. A title company will not insure, however, that after acquired title of the grantor vests in the grantee unless it is clear that certain limitations on the rule —recording laws and effect of knowledge by grantee that his grantor did not then have title—are not applicable.

14.03 QUITCLAIM DEED

A quitclaim deed may be in the same form as a grant deed, with the word "grant" changed to "quitclaim."

The word "quitclaim" conveys the title of the grantor then owned.

A deed containing the words "grant all my right, title and interest in," etc., is a quitclaim deed.

A quitclaim of an interest in a decedent's estate before distribution is a good conveyance of the interest later distributed, if the deed is executed and delivered subsequent to the date of the death of the deceased. Such quitclaim, however, would not carry the title a widow later acquired through an order assigning the estate to her under Section 645, Probate Code.

14.04 GIFT DEED

A gift deed is valid, unless made to defraud creditors, in which event it may be voided by them.

An attorney-in-fact cannot make a gift deed.

In issuing a policy of title insurance based on a gift deed, a title company will investigate the facts surrounding the deed's execution. It will go into the question of delivery, of whether or not undue influence or fraud was used, or of whether or not creditors were defrauded. If the gift deed was made within three years before the grantor died, it will consider the question of whether or not the property would be subject to the lien of federal or state taxes.

14.05 GENERAL INFORMATION

A—An **unrecorded conveyance** of real property (except a lease for a term not exceeding a year) is void as against any subsequent purchaser or mortgagee, in good faith and for value, whose conveyance is first duly recorded. However, as between the parties thereto, and any person having notice of it, an unrecorded instrument is valid.

B—A deed of **all property owned or thereafter acquired** (without specific description) is valid as to property owned at its date, but is invalid as to that subsequently acquired, since the thing granted must have either actual or potential existence, and a mere possibility cannot be transferred, although if founded on an adequate consideration, the deed may be enforceable in equity as an agreement to convey or estoppel.

C—A person may **convey to himself** and another person or other persons.

D—A deed to "John Jones or Mary Jones" or to "John Jones and/or Mary Jones" will not be insured by a title company. (But a note drawn to "John Jones or Mary Jones" is good.)

E—A deed to the "Estate of John Jones" may be treated by a title company as void, there being no grantee capable of taking title. (See Section 14.09.)

F—A deed to "John Jones and John Smith" conveys to each presumptively one-half, but this is rebuttable.

G—**Love and affection** is a good consideration, as is better maintenance and support. (See Section 14.04.)

H—Grantors **must be referred to in the body** of the deed. Their signatures alone are not sufficient. If the caption recites "The undersigned hereby grants," that is a sufficient reference to the grantors.

I—A grant is construed in favor of the grantee (except that a reservation in any grant, and every grant by a public officer or body, as such, to a private party, is interpreted in favor of the grantor).

J—The transfer of a thing **transfers also all its incidents,** unless expressly excepted. Thus a conveyance of land subject to a lease carries the right to collect the rents, and the grantee is subrogated to all rights of the grantor as a lessor. If the lease is an oil lease it is advisable that the deed specifically describe the rights under the lease that are conveyed.

K—**Re-delivering a grant to the grantor,** or canceling it, does not operate to re-transfer the title. A grant cannot be assigned.

L—**A person sentenced to a state prison for life,** or for a less term, may make and acknowledge a sale or conveyance of property.

M—**Unless there is a grantee capable of taking title** a grant is void. A deed to a "fictitious" person is void.

N—A person in whom the title to real estate is vested, who afterwards, for any cause, **has his name changed,** must, in any conveyance thereof, set forth, in addition to his present name, the name in which he derived title, and the recorder must index both names. (Also see Sections 42.01 to 42.03.)

O—A **deed purely testamentary in character** is void. This applies only when the grantor intended that the deed should not operate until his death. If a present interest passes, although only an interest in a future estate, or subject to defeat or revocation, it is valid.

(A title company, asked to insure title based on a deed that appears to be testamentary in character, will first investigate the facts surrounding the deed's execution—consideration, delivery, mental condition of grantor and possible rights of creditors and heirs.)

P—A **forged deed** is absolutely void, even in the hands of a bona fide purchaser.

Q—**Misnomer of the grantee** cannot be cured by a correction deed, although mere error in recitals may be, as in case of tax deeds or trustees' deeds.

R—**Affidavits** may be used to explain defects, but not to change them.

S—It is bad policy (although not illegal) for a grantor to sign as a **subscribing witness** to the signature by mark of another grantor in the same deed and it is even more objectionable for either spouse to sign as a **subscribing witness** to the signature of the other.

T—**An exception** in a deed withdraws from its operation some part of the thing granted, that would otherwise pass, while a **reservation** creates some new right or privilege for the benefit of the grantor in the land that is granted, which did not exist as an independent right before the grant. An exception is of some part of the thing granted and of a thing in being, and the effect is to leave the title to the thing excepted in the grantor, the same as if it had never been granted, as the retention of a designated part of the land granted, or of the timber growing on the land. A reservation is equivalent to an express grant by the grantee to the grantor, such as the retention of rents, easements, or the right to remove timber. An exception from the fee should be excepted from the description, but not so if merely an incorporeal right, such as an easement or right-of-way rather than title to the thing, has been retained. (See "Descriptions.")

U—A **deed in lieu of foreclosure** of a mortgage or deed of trust should be supported by adequate consideration. Title companies hold that this should be at least the cancellation of the indebtedness if the grantor is personally liable, and additional consideration if he is not so liable.

14.06 SIGNATURE BY MARK

Signature or subscription includes mark, when the person cannot write, his name being written near it, by a person who writes his own name as a witness; provided, that when a signature is by mark it must, in order that the same may be acknowledged or may serve as the signature to any sworn statement, be witnessed by two persons (of whom one may be the notary) who must subscribe their own names as witnesses thereto. (14, C.C.)

It is sufficient if the names of the witnesses appear near the mark **as witnesses.** However, the use of the following witness clause is advisable:

> John Smith, being unable to write, made his mark in my presence and I signed his name at his request and in his presence.

Additional Witness: _____

A deed executed by mark with only one witness is good as between the parties, but will not be passed by a title company until it has been of record for a year.

14.07 DEEDS TO OR FROM MINORS
A—Who are minors

Minors are all persons under the age of 21 years, except that any person lawfully married who is 18 or over is deemed an adult person for the purpose of entering into any engagement or transaction respecting property. Prior to 1955, the Civil Code provided that any **woman** lawfully married who is 18 or over is deemed an adult person for the foregoing purpose. (Veterans under 21 are also deemed to be adults for the purpose of purchasing homes or farms from the California Department of Veterans Affairs.)

Prior to July 29, 1927, minors were males under 21 and females under 18.

B—What is a lawful marriage

Since any person 18 or over, and under 21, who is **lawfully** married is deemed to be an adult for the purposes of dealing in property, it may be necessary in title work to determine the legality of the marriage. If the person was married outside of California, and the marriage was valid by the laws of the country in which the same was contracted, the marriage is valid in California. If the person was married in California, the age of the person will determine the procedure necessary to effect a valid marriage. (See Section 56, Civil Code.)

C—What minors may or may not do

A minor may **acquire** property.

A minor **under 18** cannot make a deed or any contract relating to real property.

A minor **over 18** may make a deed or conveyance but it may be disaffirmed by him before he becomes of age or within a reasonable time thereafter. (If the minor is married or a veteran, this statement is subject to modification. See Section 14.07-A.)

A minor's guardian may convey only upon proper order of court.

A guardian is authorized, under court supervision, to purchase, or join with the spouse of the ward or any other person or persons in the purchase, **either for cash or upon credit,** real property or some interest, equity or estate therein, in severalty, in common, in community or in joint tenancy. This is provided for in Section 1557.1, as added on May 31, 1947 to the Probate Code, a section particularly helpful to veterans under 21 who wish to obtain G.I. loans for the purchase of a home, business or farm under the Servicemen's Readjustment Act of 1944.

14.08 **DEEDS TO OR FROM INSANE OR INCOMPETENT PERSONS**

Such persons may acquire title, but cannot convey, except by a guardian or conservator acting upon due order of court.

14.09 **DEEDS TO GUARDIANS, ADMINISTRATORS, EXECU-TORS, HEIRS OR DEVISEES**

Such deeds preferably should not run to the guardian, administrator, or executor (unless the phrase "subject to the administration of the estate" is added), but should run to the **minor** or **incompetent** himself or to **the heirs or devisees of** _____ deceased, subject to the administration of the estate of said decedent.

14.10 **CONSTABLE'S OR MARSHAL'S DEED**

If proceedings leading up to a constable's or marshal's (or even a sheriff's) deed are had in a **justice's** court, the deed is not prima facie evidence of title. If in a **small claims** court, the deed may not be prima facie evidence and will not be insured.

14.11 **ACCEPTANCE OF DEEDS TO GOVERNMENTAL BODIES**

Deeds or grants conveying real estate or any interest therein or easements thereon to a political corporation or governmental agency, for public purposes, shall not be accepted for recordation without the consent of the grantee, which may be evidenced by a certificate or resolution of acceptance. (Sec. 27281, Govt. Code)

14.12 **DEEDS TO DEPARTMENT OF VETERANS AFFAIRS**

Such deeds should run to:

"Department of Veterans Affairs of the State of California." These deeds need not have a resolution of acceptance attached.

On May 20, 1946, the Department of Veterans Affairs of the State of California succeeded to the Veterans' Welfare Board of the State of California which had been created in 1921 by the Legislature. Deeds recorded after May 20, 1946, conveying property vested in the Veterans' Welfare Board must name the grantor as: "Department of Veterans Affairs of the State of California, successor to Veterans' Welfare Board."

DESCRIPTIONS
(Also see "Maps" and "Measurements")

15.01 GENERAL RULES FOR CONSTRUING DESCRIPTIONS

A—If the language is **sufficient to identify** the property, the description is a good one, and inconsistencies or even errors may be ignored.

B—**Indefinite particulars** in a description do not invalidate definite particulars.

C—**Boundaries or monuments** are paramount to lines or angles, if the latter are inconsistent with the former. Ties always overrule distances or courses.

D—**Lines** are paramount to angles, if the latter are inconsistent with the former.

E—A **map** is paramount to other particulars that are inconsistent, if it appears that the parties acted with reference to the map.

F—When a **road or non-navigable stream** of water is the boundary in a deed, the title to the center of the road or thread of the stream is conveyed (unless the title is held by a party other than the grantor.)

G—When **tide water** is the boundary in a deed, the title to the ordinary high-water mark is conveyed.

H—When a **navigable lake or stream, where there is no tide,** is the boundary, the title to the edge at low-water mark is conveyed.

I—Where there are **conflicting descriptions** of the same property, the more definite one should be given preference.

J—A **detailed metes or bounds** description will control a general one.

K—An **inaccurate statement as to acreage** in a description may be ignored, unless the language of the deed shows that only a specific quantity of land was intended to be conveyed.

L—**United States Government surveys** control and the section lines, corners and monuments thereby established are conclusive. Hence, for example, the "Northwest quarter" of a certain section is that portion established as the Northwest quarter by the located monuments, even if it is not, in area, the mathematical one-quarter of the section.

M—A reference to another deed or map has the effect of incorporating in the deed the instrument referred to.

N—If, in a description, there is a conflict between a number (of a lot, block, tract, etc.) **as spelled out** and as referred to **in figures,** the spelled-out word will prevail over the figures.

15.02 WHEN THE BOUNDARY IS A PUBLIC ROAD

A—The owner of land abutting on a road is presumed to own to the center of the road, but the contrary may be shown.

B—A deed of a lot in a subdivision showing a dedicated street adjoining will, unless a contrary intent appears, carry the title of the grantor to the center of the street, subject to the rights of the public to use the street. Even after vacation of the street, the grantor's title to the center of the vacated street will pass in a deed of this adjoining lot.

C—**Words or terms in a description that will carry title to the center of the street** (provided grantor has title):

"To the East line of 'A' Street and **thence** along 'A' Street";

"Along 'A' Street"; To or along "the street line"; To or along "the line of Lot 'B'"; "Bounded on the north by the south side of Spring Street."

D—**Words or terms in a description that ordinarily will not carry title to the center of the street:**

"To the East line of 'A' Street and **thence** along the East line of 'A' Street."

"Along the East line of 'A' Street."

Exception of "the South 10 feet within the lines of 'A' Street."

(This exception in a deed will absolutely except the fee.)

15.03 RIGHTS OF OWNER OF PROPERTY ABUTTING ON A HIGHWAY

An owner of property abutting on a public highway has a peculiar right in that highway distinct from the public, whether or not he owns the fee therein. Upon vacation he might still have the right of ingress and egress.

15.04 AREAS COMPUTED TO STREET CENTERS

A deed of the "East half of Lot A" or the "East 50 feet of Lot A," ordinarily conveys an area computed within lot lines, unless the further wording of the deed or a recital on the recorded map indicates that the area or distance is computed to the center of the street adjoining Lot A.

15.05 WHEN THE BOUNDARY IS A STREAM

A—Words or terms in a description that will carry title to the center (or thread) of the stream, provided grantor has title:

Bounded by; Running along; With the stream; Running by; To the stream; To the line of the stream; With the meander line; Fronting on; Lying along.

B—Words or terms in a description that will not carry title to the center (or thread) of the stream: The margin; The edge; The bank; The side; The east line; Outer line; Near line; To the east line of the stream.

15.06 THE WORDS "EXCEPT" AND "RESERVING" AS USED IN DESCRIPTIONS

Neither word is conclusive in determining whether or not the fee title to the portion in question is being conveyed.

15.07 WHEN DOES A DEED TO A CITY OR TO THE COUNTY FOR A ROAD CONVEY THE FEE AND WHEN AN EASEMENT

A deed will be construed to convey the fee unless it clearly appears therefrom that the intention was to grant a right-of-way or easement only. Thus a grant of land "to be used for a road" will ordinarily convey the fee, unless the words are used as a limitation upon the interest conveyed; but a grant of land as a right-of-way only creates an easement. (103 Cal. 516; 186 Cal. 151.)

(Examine the language of each deed very carefully.)

15.08 **WORDS "NORTH" OR "NORTHERLY," ETC.**

The words "north," "east," "west," and "south," unless qualified or controlled by other words, mean due north, east, west or south, and the words "northerly," "easterly," "westerly," or "southerly," where there is no object to direct inclination, mean due north, east, west or south. (96 Cal. 505.)

DIVORCE

16.01 **EFFECT ON COMMUNITY PROPERTY**

A—**When adultery, incurable insanity or extreme cruelty is the ground** the court must assign the community property to the respective parties in such proportions as it deems just. If the court fails to assign the community property, such property is subject to disposition by the court in a subsequent action or proceeding between the parties.

B—**When the grounds are other than adultery, incurable insanity or extreme cruelty,** the court must divide the community property equally between the parties and, if no disposition is made by the court, each party becomes the owner of an undivided half, in the absence of a property settlement between them.

16.02 **COMMUNITY PROPERTY ACQUIRED AFTER INTERLOCUTORY DECREE**

Property acquired by the husband, other than by gift, devise or descent, after the divorce action has been begun and before the final decree, is presumptively community property, even if acquired after the interlocutory decree.

16.03   **If there is an allegation in the complaint that there is no community property** and the decree so finds, or recites that all allegations of the complaint are true, the decree is an adjudication in accordance with the allegations of the complaint, as to any property owned by the parties at the time the action was commenced, provided defendant is served personally or has actual knowledge of the action before the decree becomes immune to direct attack, and provided no property settlement agreement changing this has been entered into.

16.04   **INTERLOCUTORY DECREE**

The interlocutory decree does not dissolve the marriage. Until entry of the final decree the parties are married.

The interlocutory decree becomes final, however, *as to property rights adjudicated therein*, under the following circumstances:

A—In a contested case, if there has been no appeal and the time for an appeal or motion for new trial has expired;

B—In a default case (on personal service) if the time has expired to vacate the decree, which would be six months after the entry of the decree. (473, C.C.P.)

A title company will not issue an owner's policy of title insurance, however, in favor of a husband or wife who acquired title under an interlocutory decree, until the entry of the final decree—unless there has been a deed from the other party. This is because the parties to the divorce might become reconciled and resume marital relations, in which event, **as between the parties**, the interlocutory decree might be nullified.

The title of a **grantee** of such husband or wife, or of a **lender**, however, can in some cases be insured.

16.05   **FINAL DECREE**

When one year has expired after the entry of the interlocutory decree, the court, on motion of either party, or upon its own motion, may enter the final judgment granting the divorce, and such final judg-

64

ment restores the parties to the status of single persons.

The death of either party after entry of the interlocutory judgment does not impair the power of the court to enter final judgment.

On the motion of either party, or upon its own motion, the court may cause a final judgment to be signed and entered, whenever such judgment had not been signed or entered, **through mistake, negligence, or inadvertence**—such final judgment to be granted **as of the date when the same could have been given** by the court if applied for. Under such circumstances the marriage of either of the parties subsequent to one year after the granting of the interlocutory judgment shall be valid.

16.06 ALIMONY

A judgment for alimony or for maintenance is a lien on real property upon the recording of an abstract thereof in the county recorder's office, provided it is for the payment of a definite and certain sum of money (even though it is payable in installments). A lien may also be impressed on specific real property by court order.

In 1959 Section 674.5 was added to the Code of Civil Procedure to provide that a certified copy of any judgment or order for alimony or child support, when recorded, shall become a lien upon all property of the judgment debtor for the respective amounts and installments as they mature.

16.07 EFFECT OF DIVORCE ON HOMESTEADS (See Homesteads, Sec. 27.22.)

16.08 SEPARATE MAINTENANCE

The court, in granting the husband or wife permanent support and maintenance, must make the same disposition of the community property and of the homestead, if any, as would have been made in a divorce action dissolving the marriage.

16.09 **ANNULMENT**

Property is not ordinarily affected by a decree annulling a marriage, unless the parties submit it as an issue.

16.10 **PROPERTY SETTLEMENT AGREEMENTS**

Agreements between a husband and wife purporting to make a settlement of present or future community rights in property will be examined by a title company with care.

When property settlements are conditional, it may be impossible for a title company to determine whether fulfillment of the conditions has been made by the parties. The language, too, must be sufficiently explicit to accomplish its purpose. Also, if the property settlement purports to affect property thereafter acquired, and the property in question comes under that classification, it will be necessary for a title company to ascertain the status of the parties and the property at the date the particular property was acquired before a vesting can be made thereunder, or a title passed based thereon. Events occurring subsequent to the execution of the settlement, such as the death, divorce or remarriage of the parties, prior to the acquisition of the property, may alter the effect of the agreement, and the status of the property may be otherwise than as agreed therein. Also it is possible that in a divorce action, or other proceeding, the property settlement agreement may have been set aside.

16.11 **FOREIGN DIVORCE**

Land in California cannot be awarded by the court of a foreign state, though the court may have power to dissolve the marriage.

EASEMENTS

17.01   Easements—rights or privileges in land distinct from the ownership of the land—may be created by grant, express or implied, or by agreement, or acquired by prescription.

They are divided, generally, into two classes, namely: easements **appurtenant** and easements **in gross**. The former is one the ownership of which is attached to a particular parcel of land. The latter is a mere personal right.

An easement is deemed appurtenant to land when it is by right used with the land for its benefit, as in the case of a right-of-way, or water-course, or a passage for light, air or heat from or across the land of another. In case of an easement appurtenant, the land to which it is attached is called the **dominant tenement,** and the land upon which a burden is laid is called the **servient tenement.** In case of an easement in gross there is no dominant tenement. Whether an easement is appurtenant or in gross is determined mainly by the nature of the right and the intention of the parties. It will not be presumed to be in gross if it can fairly be construed to be appurtenant, as where it is appropriate or useful to particular land, unless the contrary clearly appears.

ESTATE TAX
(See "Federal Estate Tax")

EXECUTIONS

18.01 **DEFINITION**

A writ issued in the name of the people, under the seal of the court, and subscribed by the clerk, or issued by a justice of the peace, directed to a sheriff, constable, marshal or commissioner appointed by the court to enforce a judgment against the property or person of a judgment debtor. (It is not to be confused with a writ of attachment which is issued prior to a judgment. See "Attachments.") A money judgment ordinarily can be enforced only by the issuance of a writ of execution.

18.02 **WITHIN WHAT TIME EXECUTION MAY ISSUE**

A—Within ten years after entry of judgment, excluding from said computation the time during which its issuance is stayed or enjoined by order of court or operation of law.

B—After ten years from entry of judgment by leave of court, upon motion and after due notice to the judgment debtor accompanied by an affidavit or affidavits setting forth sufficient reasons for failure to proceed within the ten-year period. (The code provides that a judgment in all cases may also be enforced or carried into execution after ten years from its entry by judgment for that purpose founded upon supplemental proceedings.)

18.03 **PROPERTY SUBJECT TO EXECUTION**

All property, real and personal, or any interest therein, of the judgment debtor, not exempt by law, and all property duly attached in the action. (Section 688, C.C.P.)

18.04 **PROPERTY EXEMPT FROM EXECUTION OR ATTACHMENT**

The list is a long one, beginning with chairs, tables, desks and books, to the value of $200.00, and ending with certain moneys belonging to fraternal organizations.

Reference is made to Sections 690.1 to 690.25, C.C.P., for details.

To avail himself of exemption rights, the judgment debtor or defendant must make a claim to exemption as provided by Section 690.26, C.C.P.

No article, however, or species of property, mentioned in Sections 690.1 to 690.24, inclusive, C.C.P., is exempt from execution issued upon a judgment recovered for its price, or upon a judgment of foreclosure of a mortgage or other lien thereon.

18.05 **RETURN OF EXECUTION**

The execution may be made returnable to the court in which the judgment was entered at any time not less than ten nor more than sixty days after its receipt by the officer to whom it is directed.

If an execution is returned unsatisfied, another may

be afterwards issued within the time specified in the code.

18.06 **LIEN OF EXECUTION**

A—**Effect of Judgment Lien.** The lien of an execution is distinct from the lien of a judgment. Where the judgment is a lien, there is no necessity for the formal levy of an execution, as it adds nothing to the effect of the judgment, since an execution neither creates a judgment lien, nor extends a judgment lien once created. **Hence, to preserve the priority of a judgment lien, a sale thereunder must be made during the statutory period of the judgment lien.**

B—**But where the judgment is not a lien** an execution is a lien on land from the date of its levy thereon.

C—**An execution is levied** in the same manner as an attachment—that is, by recording a copy of the writ, with a notice that the land, as described, is attached, and serving a similar notice on the occupant of the land, or if none, by posting upon the property. (688, C.C.P. See also Section 692, C.C.P.)

D—**Duration of lien.** Since July 29, 1927, a levy binds property for a period not longer than one year from the date of issuance of the execution, **except** a levy on the interests or claims of heirs, devisees or legatees in or to assets of deceased persons remaining in the hands of executors or administrators thereof prior to distribution and payment. (688, C.C.P.)

18.07 **HOW DISCHARGED OR RELEASED**

A—By a sale of the property, or by a return of the writ wholly satisfied.

B—By order of court vacating the writ or decree enjoining the enforcement of the same.

C—By a satisfaction of the judgment or proceedings voiding the judgment.

D—By a release duly recorded, executed by the judgment creditor, or his assignee, or his attorney, or by the officer who levied the execution. (See Sections 560, 688 and 716, C.C.P.)

18.08 EXECUTION AFTER DEATH OF PARTY

Notwithstanding the death of a party after judgment, execution may be issued thereon, as follows:

A—In case of the death of the judgment creditor, upon application of his executor, administrator, or successor in interest.

B—In case of the death of the judgment debtor, if the judgment is for the recovery of real or personal property or the enforcement of a lien thereon. (686, C.C.P.)

(In the case of a **money judgment,** however, the creditor must present his claim against the estate—unless he has actually levied upon the debtor's property before the debtor's death, in which event the property may be sold in satisfaction of the judgment. A title company will call for proof that the debtor was alive at the time the levy was made, when asked to insure the title to property transferred by execution sale following a money judgment. If the debtor were dead at the time of levy, the sale would be void. 730, 732, Prob.C.)

18.08a EXECUTION SALE WHEN DEBTOR INCOMPETENT OR BANKRUPT

Such sale should not be insured if the debtor has been judicially declared incompetent or when the debtor has been adjudicated bankrupt.

18.09 **Successor in Office of Sheriff** who made the sale may execute the deed pursuant thereto.

18.10 **Deed Executed Before Right of Redemption** has expired is void.

18.11 **If a Judgment is Void** for any reason, an execution, and all proceedings had thereon, are also void.

18.12 **Right of Redemption** from execution sale—see under **Foreclosure of Mortgages,** as the same rules apply.

18.13 EXECUTION, REQUEST FOR NOTICE OF SALE UNDER

Any person may file with the clerk of the court a written request that he be given notice by mailing of any sale under any execution issued upon the judgment. . . . Whenever a writ of execution is thereafter issued the clerk must note upon such writ the fact that notice has been requested and the name and address in the request. The officer who conducts a sale under the writ must mail a copy of the notice of time and place of sale to the person at the address noted. (692a, C.C.P., in effect August 27, 1937.)

FEDERAL ESTATE TAX
(Also see "Inheritance Tax—State")

19.01 **GENERAL INFORMATION**

The United States imposes a tax on the net estate of a person dying on or after September 9, 1916. This is not an inheritance tax, and is not computed on the amount of each inheritance as is the California tax, but is a tax computed on the total net value of the estate, regardless of the number of persons or the relationship of the persons by whom the estate is acquired, and is in addition to the state tax.

It attaches to property transferred within three years of death without adequate consideration, trusts and transfers made in contemplation of death, interests in joint tenancies and assets generally. It follows the property even after a probate sale.

A flat **exemption** of $60,000.00 is allowed to the estate ·(including life insurance) of a resident of the United States. In addition thereto, funeral and administration expenses, claims against the estate and other similar charges are allowed as deductions. (If the decedent died after August 30, 1935, and prior to the amendment on October 21, 1942, the exemption was $40,000.00. If the decedent died after June 6, 1932, and prior to the amendment on August 30, 1935, the exemption was $50,000.00. If he died after February 26, 1926, and prior to the amendment of June 6, 1932, the exemption was $100,000.00. If he died prior to the amendment of February 26, 1926, the exemption was $50,000.00.)

19.02 **LIEN OF TAX**

The lien of the tax attaches immediately upon death. Unless sooner paid in full, the tax remains a lien for ten years upon the gross estate of the decedent, except such part thereof as is used for the payment of charges against the estate and expenses of administration allowed by any court having jurisdiction thereof. The lien follows the property into the possession of distributees or purchasers.

FEDERAL GIFT TAX
(Also see "State Gift Tax")

20.01 **GENERAL INFORMATION**

This is a federal tax imposed upon the transfer of property by gift. It applies to transfers made after June 6, 1932.

The rate (effective October 21, 1942) is three-fourths of the federal estate tax rate.

The exemptions are: (1) $3000.00 of gifts in each year to each donee; (2) gifts for charitable, religious and educational purposes; and (3) $30,000.00 of gifts to all donees in all years combined.

The donor is required to file a return with the collector of internal revenue in his district on or before March 15th following the close of the calendar year. At that time, also, the tax is payable by the donor.

20.02 **LIEN OF TAX**

This gift tax is a lien upon all gifts made during the calendar year. If it is not paid when due, the donee is personally liable therefor. The lien remains for 10 years from the date of the gift unless the tax is paid or unless the donee makes a sale to a bona fide purchaser. In the latter case the lien falls on the other property of the donee, including that after acquired.

FEDERAL TAX LIENS

21.01 **GENERAL INFORMATION**

Under Section 3186 U.S. Revised Statutes, as amended, any internal revenue tax, unpaid after demand, becomes a lien on **all property and rights to**

property of the person liable therefor, from the time the assessment is made by an assessment officer appointed by the District Director, valid, however, against any mortgagee, purchaser or judgment creditor only when notice thereof is filed in the county recorder's office.

A title company will report federal tax liens not only against the person in title, **but against** the husband or wife of the person in title—unless the title stood of record as the title holder's separate property prior to the date when the assessment list was received by the internal revenue collector.

21.02 **FEDERAL TAX LIENS IN CASE OF MORTGAGE OR TRUST DEED FORECLOSURE**

A—In **actions** brought to quiet title to, or for the foreclosure of a mortgage, trust deed or lien upon, real estate or personal property, the United States may be made a defendant—**for the purpose of adjudicating any lien or claim of the United States.** (See Section 22.08.) Where the United States is a party defendant, the redemption period shall, as to it, in all cases and regardless of sale price, be deemed to be one year.

B—Prior to 1960 the rule was followed that after a **trustee's sale** upon foreclosure, a federal tax lien against the former owner might not be disregarded without:

(a) A release or certificate of discharge being filed in the recorder's office by the collector or director of internal revenue; or

(b) An adjudication by the District Court of the United States following the filing of a bill in equity.

C—Following the decision of the United States Supreme Court in Bank of America v. U.S. and Brosnan v. U.S., 4 L.Ed. 2d 1192 (June 13, 1960), the rule was adopted that a junior federal tax lien was extinguished as a lien against real property by the exercise of a power of sale by the trustee under a prior deed of trust.

73

FORECLOSURE OF MORTGAGES
(Also see "Mortgages"; "Deficiency Judgments";
"Moratorium"; and "Trust Deed Foreclosure")

22.01 **THE ACTION TO FORECLOSE IN GENERAL**

The necessary parties to a mortgage foreclosure action are the owner and those persons **shown by the records** to have an interest or lien **inferior** to the mortgage.

A foreclosure action affects only the property on which the mortgage is a valid lien. Regardless of who are made defendants, the action **does not quiet title**. A purchaser at a foreclosure sale acquires only the mortgagor's title.

A decree of foreclosure is good only against those persons properly made parties who are duly served or appear.

Following the decree of foreclosure (and after due notice of sale), the sheriff or commissioner sells the property to the highest bidder. The purchaser gets a **certificate of sale**, evidence that he has acquired the legal title to the property, subject to certain redemption rights. If twelve months pass, without redemption having been made, the purchaser is entitled to a deed from the sheriff or commissioner. If the sale is for the full amount of the obligation, the period of redemption is 3 months.

22.02 **NOTICE OF ACTION**

To be effective the notice of action must contain the names of all the parties who are made defendants. From the time of its filing for record any purchaser or encumbrancer of the property affected is deemed to have constructive notice of the pendency of the action.

Encumbrances filed, recorded or docketed **after the notice of action to foreclose has been recorded**, will be ignored by a title company in its policy, if the sheriff's or commissioner's deed upon foreclosure is of record. The same is true of deeds executed by the

74

mortgagor (or his successors in interest) **after** the re-cording of the mortgage in question and placed of rec-ord **after** the filing of the notice of action. But if no notice of action has been recorded, encumbrances or deeds subsequent to and recorded during the action cannot be ignored, even if the sheriff's or commission-er's deed is of record, unless the parties are sued. The notice of action must contain the name of the owner at the date of its filing or it will not be effective as to his successors.

22.03 **REDEMPTION**

Sales of **personal property** are absolute, as are sales of a leasehold of two years unexpired term.

In all other cases the **property is subject to redemp-tion** by the following persons, or their successors in interest.

A—The **judgment debtor,** or his successor in inter-est, in the whole or any part of the property.

B—A **creditor** having a lien by judgment or mort-gage on the property sold, or some part thereof, sub-sequent to that under which the property was sold. A redemption by such person operates as an assignment of the certificate of sale and a sheriff's or commission-er's deed will issue to him if no further redemption is made within the time allowed by law.

Redemption by the judgment debtor, or his succes-sor in interest, terminates the sale. A certificate of re-demption is issued to him.

Prior to February 26, 1897, the debtor had six months from the date of the sheriff's sale to redeem. Since that date the redemption period has been **twelve months.** (See Section 22.01 where period may be three months.)

Partial redemption cannot be made unless the par-cels are sold separately.

On redemption **by the debtor** the lien of a deficiency judgment that has been obtained against him will at-tach. (This does not apply if redemption is made by his successor in interest.)

A **sheriff's deed** issued before expiration of the right of redemption is void.

If no redemption is made, the sheriff or commissioner, upon request, will issue a deed to the purchaser or his assignee. (A reference to an assignment of the certificate of sale in the sheriff's deed is sufficient; the assignment need not be of record.)

If a certificate of redemption is issued to the **debtor or his successor in interest** all encumbrances which would have been cut out by the issuance of a sheriff's or commissioner's deed will be shown by a title company in its policy. Redemption by him leaves the title in the same condition in which it would have been if no suit had been brought, except that the mortgage is discharged.

22.04 **REINSTATEMENT OF MORTGAGE PRIOR TO DECREE OF FORECLOSURE**

(See Section 58.18.)

22.05 **WHEN A MORTGAGOR COMES BACK INTO TITLE FOLLOWING A FORECLOSURE**

(See Section 41.10.)

22.06 **THE STATE AS A PARTY IN FORECLOSURE ACTIONS**

In all actions brought to foreclose a **deed of trust, mortgage or other lien** on real property upon which exists a lien to secure the payment of taxes to the State of California, other than taxes upon such real property, the State of California may be made a party and the priority of such liens determined. Service of summons shall be upon the secretary of state or his assistant, or any of his deputies, and upon the attorney general, or any of his deputies. (Section 2931a, C.C.) A copy of the complaint shall be delivered to the officer, board, commission, department or division or other body charged with the collection of the tax or obligation.

In all actions brought to foreclose a **mortgage, deed of trust or other lien** on real property upon which exists an old age aid lien, the State of California may be made a party. Service of summons shall be upon the chairman of the board of supervisors for the county and upon the director of the department of social welfare for the state.

22.07 **DEFICIENCY JUDGMENTS**
(See Section 31.10.)

22.08 **UNITED STATES OF AMERICA AS A PARTY DEFENDANT**

The United States may be named as a party defendant if it has a mortgage or other lien upon the property. Service is made by delivery of a copy of summons and complaint to the United States Attorney for the district in which the action is brought, or to an Assistant United States Attorney or clerical employee designated by the United States Attorney in a writing filed with the clerk of the court, and by sending a copy of the summons and of complaint by registered mail to the Attorney General of the United States at Washington, D.C.

FOREIGN ADMINISTRATORS, EXECUTORS OR GUARDIANS
Their power to release mortgages

23.01   Foreign executors, administrators and guardians may satisfy mortgages upon the records of any county in this state, upon producing and recording in the office of the county recorder of the county in which such mortgage is recorded, a duly certified and authenticated copy of their letters testamentary, or of administration or guardianship, and which certificate or authentication shall also recite that said letters have not been revoked.

It is advisable that the release of the mortgage should bear a date shortly prior to the date of authentication and certification.

FOREIGN LANGUAGE INSTRUMENTS

24.01 An instrument written in a foreign language may be recorded by attaching thereto an English translation (certified as true by a judge of a court of record). The recorder will accept and permanently file the same and will record the certified translation.

On and after September 22, 1951, in those counties where photostatic or photographic method of recording is employed, the whole instrument, including the foreign language and the translation may be recorded, and the original instrument returned to the party leaving it for record or upon his order. (Section 27293, Gov't Code.)

FOREIGN SIGNATURE

25.01 When an instrument is signed in Hebrew, German or other alien characters, it should show a witness opposite signature and state:

Witness to signature of _____,
who signs in (Hebrew, etc.).

FORGERY

26.01 A forged instrument is void even in the hands of an innocent purchaser or encumbrancer.

GIFT TAX
(See "Federal Gift Tax" and "State Gift Tax")

HOMESTEADS

27.01 **DEFINITION**

The homestead consists of the dwelling house in which the claimant resides, together with outbuildings, and the land on which they are situated, selected in the statutory method.

When a declaration of homestead has been filed in the recorder's office, containing the statements required by statute, provided the same are true, the property becomes a homestead, protected from execution and forced sale, except as otherwise provided by statute, and remains so until conveyed, or abandoned by a recorded instrument of abandonment. (Prior to 1860 a declaration was unnecessary, residence being the only requirement.)

27.02 **A HOMESTEAD MAY BE CLAIMED BY:**

A—The head of a family—the homestead claim not to exceed $12,500 in actual cash value, over and above all liens and encumbrances on the property at the time of any levy of execution thereon.

B—Any other person—the homestead claim not to exceed $5000 in actual cash value over and above all liens and encumbrances. (See Sections 27.03 and 27.04.)

C—In 1959, provision was made for a "married person's separate homestead." Following a decree of separate maintenance or an interlocutory decree of divorce, each spouse may declare a homestead from his or her separate property or any property awarded by the decree. (See Section 27.24.)

27.03 **WHO IS THE HEAD OF A FAMILY**

A—The husband, when the claimant is a married person. (If the husband has made no declaration, the wife may declare a homestead, she being entitled to the same claim as the head of the family. 11 Cal. App. 622.)

B—Every person who has residing on the premises with him or her, and under his or her care and maintenance, either:

   (a) His or her minor child, or minor grandchild, or the minor child of his or her deceased wife or husband;

   (b) A minor brother or sister, or the minor child of a deceased brother or sister;

79

(c) A father, mother, grandfather or grandmother, either of himself or herself or of a deceased husband or wife;

(d) An unmarried sister or any of the other relatives above mentioned who have reached majority, and are unable to take care of or support themselves.

27.04 MODE OF SELECTION

The husband or other head of a family **(or in case the husband has not made such selection, the wife),** or any person other than the head of a family, must execute and acknowledge (personally), in the same manner as a grant of real property is acknowledged, a declaration of homestead, and record the same in the office of the recorder of the county in which the land is situated. If the land is partly in one county and partly in another duplicates of the declaration may be recorded, one in each county. **The date of recording the declaration** is the material date, as it is ineffective until recorded.

27.05 REQUIREMENTS OF THE DECLARATION (the omission of any of which renders the homestead void.)

A—A statement showing that claimant is the head of a family, if such is the case; or, when the declaration is made by the wife, showing that her husband has not made such declaration and that she therefore makes it for their joint benefit.

B—If claimant is married, the name of the other spouse.

C—A statement that the claimant is residing on the premises and claims them as a homestead.

D—A description of the premises (such as would be good in a deed).

E—An estimate of their actual cash value.

NOTE: The declaration **may** further contain a verified statement of the character of the property sought to be homesteaded, showing the improvements affixed thereto, with sufficient detail to show it a proper subject of homestead, etc. (See Paragraph 5 of Section

1263, Civil Code.) If so made, such statements are prima facie evidence of the truth thereof and conclusive in favor of a good faith purchaser or encumbrancer for value.

A "married person's separate homestead" must contain special recitals. (See Section 27.24.)

27.06 VALIDITY OF A HOMESTEAD

Even though the declaration may be sufficient in that it conforms with statutory requirements, the homestead may be invalid in fact, because the statements contained in the declaration are not true. From the records alone the validity of a homestead cannot be finally determined. As against attaching or judgment creditors it is usually necessary to obtain a judicial determination as to the truth of the statements contained in the declaration.

27.07 PROPERTY FROM WHICH A HOMESTEAD MAY BE SELECTED

If the claimant be married, the homestead may be selected from the community property or the separate property of the husband, or, **subject to the provisions of section 1239, from the property held by the spouses as tenants in common or in joint tenancy or from the separate property of the wife.** When the claimant is not married, but is the head of a family, within the meaning of Section 1261, the homestead may be selected from any of his or her property. If the claimant be an unmarried person, other than the head of a family, the homestead may be selected from any of his or her property. "Property" includes any freehold title, interest, or estate which vests in the claimant the immediate right of possession, even though such a right of possession is not exclusive. (1238, C.C., as amended August 27, 1937.) Section 1239, referred to, provides that the homestead cannot be selected from the separate property of the wife, without her consent, shown by her making or joining in making a declaration.

(A freehold is an estate of inheritance, an estate for life or an estate during the life of a third person.)

27.08 **HOMESTEAD ON JOINT TENANCY PROPERTY OF HUSBAND AND WIFE**

A declaration on joint tenancy property by the wife alone is valid.

A declaration by the husband on joint tenancy property requires—at least since August 27, 1937—the consent of the wife, such consent to be shown "by her making or joining in making the declaration."

27.09 **HOMESTEAD ON PROPERTY OF HUSBAND AND WIFE HELD UNDER A TENANCY IN COMMON**

A declaration on such property by the wife alone is valid.

A declaration on such property by the husband, without the wife's consent, is ineffective as to any interest which is the separate property of the wife.

27.10 **ONE HOMESTEAD AT A TIME**

A person can have only one valid homestead at a time.

27.11 **A HOMESTEAD DOES NOT DEFEAT:**

A—Judgments which became liens before the declaration was recorded.

B—Liens of mechanics, laborers, materialmen, contractors, sub-contractors, artisans, architects, builders or vendors upon the premises.

C—Mortgages and trust deeds executed and acknowledged by the husband and wife, or by an unmarried claimant.

D—Mortgages and trust deeds recorded before the declaration was recorded.

E—Federal tax liens.

27.12 **A VALID HOMESTEAD DOES DEFEAT:**

A—Money judgments which became liens after the declaration was recorded, and state tax liens having only the force and effect of a money judgment.

B—Unrecorded mortgages, not executed and acknowledged by both husband and wife, as required by statute, even though declarant had notice thereof.

C—Attachments, provided the declaration was recorded prior to the judgments rendered thereon becoming liens. (But see 5.04.)

D—An execution (unless the judgment is a valid lien on the homestead), provided the declaration was recorded prior to the sale on execution. (7 Cal. (2) 213.)

Such judgments, attachments, executions or mortgages ordinarily will not be ignored by a title company, however, but will be shown until the validity of the homestead has been upheld by judicial determination, as by quiet title decree or by order exempting the homestead obtained in a bankruptcy court.

27.13 HOMESTEAD IN EXCESS OF VALUE PERMITTED BY STATUTE

A judgment, not otherwise a lien on homestead property, does not become a lien thereon because the homesteaded property exceeds the statutory value of $12,500 for the head of a family, or $5000 for any other person.

The excess above the statutory valuation can be reached by the judgment creditor only by proceedings taken by him in accordance with the statute, which requires that, within sixty days after an execution is levied on the homestead, he apply to the Superior Court for the appointment of appraisers; otherwise the lien of the execution shall cease at the expiration of said period, and no execution based upon the same judgment shall thereafter be levied upon the homestead.

A division, or sale, of the homestead, under court order, may follow the appraisers' report. If a sale is made, the proceeds must be applied first to the discharge of all liens and encumbrances, if any, on the property, then to the homestead claimant to the amount of the homestead exemption, third to the satisfaction of the execution, and the balance, if any, to the homestead claimant.

27.14 INCREASE IN VALUE

The statutory limitation of valuation of a homestead applies at its inception, and if it enhances in value thereafter cannot exceed that amount, but every increase in value works at a reduction in area, until further reduction is impossible, when it may be sold, and the exemption be deducted from the proceeds.

27.15 APPLICATION OF PROCEEDS ON FORECLOSURE SALE

Where a homestead is mortgaged or is declared upon land subject to a mortgage, on a foreclosure sale under the mortgage the proceeds will be applied:

1st, to satisfy the mortgage debt;

2nd, to the payment of the value of the homestead exemption;

3rd, to the payment of the claim of a subsequent judgment creditor who has taken the necessary statutory proceedings for appraisal.

27.16 TO CONVEY OR ENCUMBER A HOMESTEAD

Section 1242 of the Civil Code, as amended, provides:

"The homestead of a married person cannot be conveyed or encumbered unless the instrument by which it is conveyed or encumbered is executed and acknowledged by both husband and wife or unless each spouse executes and acknowledges a separate instrument so conveying or encumbering the homestead in favor of the same party or his successor in interest; provided, however, that a conveyance of the homestead between husband and wife need be executed and acknowledged only by the spouse conveying, and unless the one conveying expressly reserves his homestead rights, the spouse to whom the conveyance is made may convey or encumber the homestead property in the manner and to the same extent as though no homestead had been declared."

Such a conveyance from one spouse to the other does not abandon the homestead, which remains exempt from forced sale. Also, any deed or encumbrance executed by the grantee in such a conveyance must be dated and acknowledged **after** that conveyance.

27.17 WHERE SPOUSE IS INSANE OR INCOMPETENT

Where real property or any interest therein is owned by husband and wife as community property or where real property or any interest therein is owned as community or separate property and is subject to a homestead and one or both of the spouses is incompetent, it may be sold and conveyed or encumbered, transferred, or exchanged or otherwise disposed of in the manner provided in Sections 1435.1 et seq., Probate Code.

(These Sections supersede the former Sections 1435 to 1435.10 of the Probate Code which in turn superseded Sections 172b, 172c, 172d, 1269a, 1269b and 1269c of the Civil Code.)

Under said Probate Code Sections, the court may, in the proceeding provided for, judicially establish the fact of incompetency or insanity, the fact that the property is community, or the fact that a homestead is valid.

Prior to 1959 the procedure above mentioned was exclusive, but since 1959 the Probate Code provides for an alternative procedure to be followed in a guardianship or conservatorship proceeding.

27.18 PROCEEDS OF SALE ARE EXEMPT

If the homestead is sold by the owner, the proceeds arising from such sale, to the extent of the value allowed for a homestead exemption, are exempt to such owner for a period of six months following.

Real property purchased with these proceeds within the six months period may be selected as a homestead and such selection, when the declaration has been filed for record, "shall have the same effect as if it had been created at the time the prior declaration of homestead was filed for record." (1265a, C.C., added September 19, 1939.)

(A purchaser at any execution sale, other than a sale pursuant to a mortgage, deed of trust or mechanic's lien foreclosure decree, will not be insured by a title company until the sheriff's or commissioner's deed has been recorded, and not then if a declaration of homestead by the judgment debtor, describing the real property as purchased with said proceeds, was recorded on or after September 19, 1939.)

27.19 **ABANDONMENT OF HOMESTEAD**

A—Section 1243 of the Civil Code, as amended September 22, 1951, provides:

"A homestead can be abandoned only by a declaration of abandonment, or a grant thereof as provided by Section 1242, executed and acknowledged:

"1. By the husband and wife, jointly or by separate instruments, if the claimant is married;

"2. By the claimant, if unmarried."

Said Section 1243 was amended in 1959 to provide that a married person's separate homestead may be abandoned by a declaration of abandonment or conveyance by the claimant alone.

Such declaration of abandonment or grant must be **recorded** before the abandonment is effective.

B—A property settlement between husband and wife may abandon a homestead.

C—Removal from the premises does not abandon the homestead.

D—A deed which is in fact a mortgage does not destroy the homestead—except as to innocent parties relying on the records. Nor does a transfer without consideration followed by a re-transfer. A reconveyance to one of the spouses under a trust deed does not destroy the homestead.

E—A declaration of abandonment does not validate **prior deeds or instruments** purporting to affect the homestead when they were not executed with the required formalities.

(Also see Section 27.16)

27.20 **EFFECT OF DEATH ON HOMESTEAD**

If the selection of the homestead was made by a married person from the community property, or from the separate property of the spouse making the selection or joining therein, or from property held in joint tenancy, the land so selected on the death of either spouse vests in the survivor, still retaining its homestead character. (But see Section 27.21.)

In other cases, upon the death of the person whose property was selected as a homestead, it goes to the heirs or devisees of such person, subject to the power of the superior court to assign the same for a limited period to the family of the decedent.

Amendments to Section 1265, Civil Code, and Sections 660 and 663, Probate Code, effective September 22, 1951, provide that if one spouse conveys the homestead property to the other without expressly reserving the homestead rights, the property vests in the heirs or devisees of the grantee spouse, subject to the power of the superior court to assign it for a limited period to the family of the decedent.

27.21 **ESTABLISHING THE DEATH OF HUSBAND OR WIFE (PARTY TO A HOMESTEAD)**

A—**If the record owner survives:** The fact of the death may be proved by:

(a) Probate proceedings in connection with other property.

(b) Special proceedings under Sections 1170 to 1175 Probate Code.

(c) A certified copy of death certificate accompanied by an affidavit of identity.

B—**If the record owner dies.** The homestead should be set apart by order of court obtained under Section 660, Probate Code—unless the homestead had been selected out of the separate property of the deceased husband without his consent, in which event there should be other appropriate court proceedings.

27.22 **EFFECT OF DIVORCE ON HOMESTEAD**

If a homestead has been selected from the **community property,** it may be assigned to the party to whom the divorce is granted, or, in cases where a divorce is granted upon the ground of incurable insanity, to the party against whom the divorce is granted. The assignment may be either absolutely or for a limited period, subject, in the latter case, to the future disposition of the court, or it may, in the discretion of the court, be divided, or be sold and the proceeds divided.

If a homestead has been selected from the **separate property** of either, in cases in which the decree is rendered upon any ground other than incurable insanity, it shall be assigned to the former owner of such property, subject to the power of the court to assign it for a limited period to the party to whom the divorce is granted; and in cases where the decree is rendered upon the ground of incurable insanity, it shall be assigned to the former owner of such property, subject to the power of the court to assign it to the party against whom the divorce is granted for a term of years not to exceed the life of such party.

If no assignment is made the homestead vests absolutely in the former owner, when the final decree is entered, even though there are minor children (182 Cal. 765).

In any event a **final decree** is necessary, since the usual rule applies that the interlocutory decree alone does not vest property rights.

27.23 PROBATE HOMESTEAD

A—Defined:

A homestead created by order of the probate court out of the property of decedent for the benefit of the surviving husband, wife or minor children of decedent, no declaration of homestead having been recorded, or the homestead having been selected by the survivor out of the separate property of decedent, the decedent not having joined therein.

B—If created out of community property, it vests as follows:

(a) In the surviving spouse, if there are no minor children.

(b) In the surviving spouse one-half and in the minor child (or children), one-half.

(c) In the minor child (or children), if there is no surviving spouse.

As each child comes of age, the homestead ceases to exist as to him, but he retains his interest in the property and may convey or encumber his interest, subject to the rights of the other children or surviving spouse. The surviving spouse likewise may convey or encumber. A minor child's interest may be sold by his guardian, pursuant to court order.

If a mortgage on the interest of one is foreclosed, the purchaser becomes a tenant in common with the other owners subject to their homestead rights, but with no right to possession until such homestead rights terminate.

When the youngest child reaches majority the property may be conveyed clear of its homestead character, provided the surviving spouse, if any, joins therein.

C—If created out of separate property, it exists for a limited period only (but not beyond the lifetime of the surviving spouse, nor beyond the child's majority), the title vesting in the heirs or devisees, subject to the effect of the limited probate homestead. But if the court sets it aside absolutely such order is valid on collateral attack. (127 Cal. 275.)

27.24 MARRIED PERSON'S SEPARATE HOMESTEAD

The declaration of a married person's separate homestead must contain a statement that the declarant is a married person, and that there is in existence a decree of separate maintenance or an interlocutory decree of divorce between declarant and his or her spouse, a statement showing that declarant is the head of a family, if such is the case, and certain other nonconflicting statements, including the optional verified information referred to in Section 24.05.

INCOME TAX
(See "State Personal Income Tax")

INHERITANCE TAX
(Also see "Federal Estate Tax")

28.01 HISTORICAL

The original act, passed in 1893, took effect March 23, 1893. It was amended in subsequent years. Prior to the amendment of 1905, in effect July 1, 1905, only collateral heirs were subject to tax. By amendment effective July 27, 1917, the wife's half of the community property was not subject to tax. The Inheritance Tax Act of 1935 went into effect June 25, 1935, at 5 o'clock P.M. On July 1, 1945, it became part of the Revenue and Taxation Code. (See Sections 13301 et seq.) In 1961 the wife was given the same exemption as the husband.

28.02 **THE TAX MAY ATTACH AS A LIEN TO:**

A—Property acquired by the survivor in the case of a joint tenancy.

B—Property transferred by deed, assignment or gift made without adequate consideration in contemplation of the death of the grantor, assignor or donor, or intended to take effect at or after such death. (As in the case of a deed made between relatives to avoid administration.) A transfer of property made more than three years prior to the death of the transferor will not be deemed (for the purposes of inheritance taxes) to be made in contemplation of death—through amendment on September 22, 1951 of Section 13642 of the Revenue and Taxation Code.

C—Property passing through probate—in which case the tax is payable to the county treasurer, in course of administration.

D—Property acquired by the remainderman in the case of the death of the holder of a life estate created by a deed in which the grantor conveys the land but reserves a life estate in himself.

28.02a **RELEASE OR SUBORDINATION OF LIEN**

The State Controller, the Inheritance Tax Attorney or a subordinate inheritance tax attorney has the power to release real property from the lien of the inheritance tax or to subordinate the lien to other liens or encumbrances. Upon the finding that no tax is due, an inheritance tax appraiser also has power—since September 9, 1953—to issue a release. The certificates of these officers, when recorded, enable title companies to ignore the possibility of lien. (Sections 14307, 14308, Rev. & Tax. Code)

28.03 EXEMPTIONS FROM THE TAX TO RELATIVES OF DECEDENT

$24,000.00 to the widow (prior to September 15, 1961)

(If however, the decedent died prior to June 25, 1935, and on or after October 25, 1933, the widow's exemption was $25,000. Prior to October 25, 1933, and on and after August 14, 1929, it was $50,000. Prior to August 14, 1929, and on or after July 1, 1911, it was $24,000.) Since September 15, 1961 the widow's exemption is $5,000.00, the same as the husband.

$12,000.00 to minor child

(If, however, the decedent died prior to June 25, 1935, and on or after July 1, 1911, the minor child's exemption was $24,000.)

$5000.00 to the husband or wife, an adult child, a grandchild, a parent, a grandparent

(If, however, the decedent died prior to June 25, 1935, the exemption of each, except the wife, was $10,000.)

$2000.00 to a brother, a sister, or a descendant of either, a wife or widow of a son, the husband of a daughter, the widower of a daughter

(If, however, the decedent died prior to June 25, 1935, and on or after August 14, 1929, the exemption of each was $5000. Prior to August 14, 1929, it was $2000.)

$500.00 to an uncle, an aunt, or a descendant of either

(If, however, the decedent died prior to June 25, 1935, and on or after August 8, 1915, the exemption of each was $1000.)

$50.00 to others

(If, however, the decedent died prior to June 25, 1935, the exemption of each was $500.)

28.04 **OTHER EXEMPTIONS**

A—On and after July 27, 1917, and prior to September 15, 1961, **the widow's half of community property** was not subject to tax, and she might receive the amount of the exemption in addition thereto without paying any tax thereon. The **surviving husband** retains **all the community property** free of tax. After September 15, 1961 the community property is exempt as to both spouses.

B—All proceeds of any federal war risk insurance policy of any veteran of World War I or World War II which is, or may become, payable to the estate of such veteran, is exempt.

C—All property transferred to this state or to the United States or to societies, corporations and institutions exempted by law from taxation, or to any public corporation, or to societies, corporations, etc., engaged in or devoted to any charitable, educational, public or other like work, or to any person, society, corporation, etc., in trust for any like purpose, **is exempt;** provided such society, corporation, etc., is organized or existing under the laws of this state or of the United States or the property is limited for use within this state, unless there are exemptions or reciprocal provisions under the laws of the foreign state or country.

D—All property transferred by a decedent to a husband, wife, lineal ancestor, lineal issue or adopted child, **provided** it was transferred to such decedent not more than five years prior to his death by another decedent in the same group of individuals **and provided** a tax was paid to the State of California.

28.05 **PROPERTY TAXABLE AND DEDUCTIONS**

Subject to the exemptions enumerated above, the tax applies, in general, to all property passing from any resident by will or the law of descent, or homestead law of this state, or by transfer without adequate consideration made in contemplation of or to take effect on death, and upon all property within this state so passing from any non-resident, subject to the following deductions:

Debts of decedent owing at date of death; expenses of last illness and funeral expenses; state, county and municipal taxes which are a lien at date of death; ordinary expenses of administration, including ordinary fees of executors and administrators and their attorneys; federal estate tax, and the amount of inheritance tax paid to any other state or foreign country, subject to certain limitations.

28.06 **PROBATE SALES, MORTGAGES AND LEASES**

Where property is sold, exchanged, or otherwise transferred under and in accordance with the provisions of the Probate Code, the lien of the inheritance tax is released from such property and attaches to the proceeds thereof.

Where property is mortgaged, hypothecated, or leased under and in accordance with the provisions of the Probate Code, the lien of the inheritance tax is subject and subordinate to the rights and interests so secured or created, the lien attaching to the proceeds of any such mortgage, hypothecation or lease.

IRRIGATION DISTRICTS

29.01   The procedure for the formation of these districts, their internal organization, powers and purposes, bonds, assessments, etc., is found in the Water Code, Sections 20500-29978.

JOINT TENANCY
(Also see "**Inheritance Tax—State**"; and "**Federal Estate Tax**")

30.01 **DEFINITION**

An estate held by two or more persons jointly, which, upon the death of one, vests in the survivor or survivors, until there is but one survivor, whereupon it vests in such survivor absolutely.

30.02 SURVIVORSHIP

The distinguishing feature is the right of survivorship. It is unnecessary, however, to accompany the creation of the joint tenancy with a declaration regarding survivorship, since it follows as a legal incident.

If one of the parties dies, he merely drops out of the title and his interests ceases, the title remaining vested in the survivor or survivors under the original deed, since the theory of survivorship is that the fee title as a whole is vested in each of the tenants, subject to the life estate of the others, and not that any title is derived by the survivor from his deceased cotenant. Nevertheless, while living, their interests may be severed.

30.03 CREATION

Section 683 of the Civil Code, as amended September 7, 1955, relating to joint tenancy, provides:

A joint interest is one owned by two or more persons in equal shares, by a title created by a single will or transfer, when expressly declared in the will or transfer to be a joint tenancy, or by transfer from a sole owner to himself and others, or from tenants in common or joint tenants to themselves or some of them, or to themselves or any of them and others, or from a husband and wife, when holding title as community property or otherwise to themselves or to themselves and others or to one of them and to another or others, when expressly declared in the transfer to be a joint tenancy, or when granted or devised to executors or trustees as joint tenants. A joint tenancy in personal property may be created by a written transfer, instrument or agreement. Provisions of this section shall not restrict the creation of a joint tenancy in a bank deposit as provided for in the Bank Act.

To create a joint tenancy at common law, four unities were required, namely: unity of time, title, interest and possession. That is, the parties must have one and the same interest, **accruing by one and the same conveyance,** commencing at one and the same time, and the property must be held by one and the same undivided possession. If any one of these unities were lacking, the estate was not a joint tenancy.

It is necessary that there be some operative words declaring the intention to create a joint tenancy.

30.04 JOINT TENANCIES CREATED BY DIRECT TRANSFER

A—From August 14, 1929, up to but not including August 14, 1931, it was permissible to create a joint tenancy "by transfer from a sole owner to himself and others, or from tenants in common to themselves, or to themselves and others." A sole owner is usually held to be one who holds his title as separate property.

B—Prior to August 14, 1929, and from August 14, 1931, up to but not including September 15, 1935, it was not possible to create a joint tenancy by direct transfer from a person to himself and others, or from tenants in common to themselves or to themselves and others.

C—Between September 15, 1935 and September 7, 1955, joint tenancies could be created by direct transfer only in so far as Section 683 C.C. then provided for them.

(If the title stands in the name of a married man or married woman, a title company will insist that a deed executed on or after September 15, 1935, by said owner to himself or herself and the other spouse as **joint tenants,** must be joined in by both husband and wife—unless the property is unquestionably separate property. Not only should both sign and acknowledge, but the names of both must appear in the preamble.)

30.05 FORM OF CONVEYANCE TO CREATE JOINT TENANCY

A joint tenancy may be created by a joint tenancy deed from the owner or owners to two or more other parties; it may be created by the owners deeding to an intermediary and taking back a joint tenancy deed; and, under certain circumstances, owners may create for themselves a joint tenancy by direct transfer. (See Section 30.04)

The intention must be clearly expressed in the granting clause in the deed without any conflicting terms. The phrase "as joint tenants" implies the right of survivorship and is sufficient. The habendum clause in the deed should not be in conflict with the granting clause. Proportionate shares must not be named, else a tenancy in common will be created.

A mortgage and the note secured thereby are ordinarily construed as one instrument, but as regards joint tenancy, both should refer to the parties as joint tenants, or, at least, the note should, it being the primary obligation.

30.06 PROPERTY AND INTERESTS AFFECTED

A joint tenancy may be created in an estate in fee, for life, for years, or in remainder. Both real and personal property, or an undivided interest therein, may be held in joint tenancy.

30.07 SEVERANCE

A conveyance by one tenant to a third party of "an undivided one-half interest," or of "all his interest," or a sheriff's or commissioner's deed, or bankruptcy proceedings, as to the interest of one of the parties, or a partition of the property, dissolves the joint tenancy, and the owners hold as tenants in common—except that if more than two persons comprise the joint tenancy, those remaining hold their interest as joint tenants as to each other and as tenants in common as to the stranger coming into the title.

One joint tenant may mortgage his interest in the property or execute a trust deed covering the same. The execution of a mortgage by one joint tenant does not sever the joint tenancy. (People v. Nogarr, 164 C.A. 2d 591)

A lease by one joint tenant is not void but passes to the lessee, during its term, the lessor's right of possession without depriving the other joint tenants of their right of possession or share of the rentals and probably without severing the joint tenancy.

Where title is in husband and wife as joint tenants, they may convert the tenancy into community property or into a tenancy in common by the execution by both of them of an *agreement* for that express purpose. This is severance of joint tenancy by agreement. A joint tenancy may also be severed by will. (Chase v. Leiter, 96 C.A. 2d 439)

30.08 TERMINATION OF JOINT TENANCY BY DEATH

When one tenant dies, proof of his death must be established of record. This may be done by (a) recording a certified copy of the death certificate, accompanied by an affidavit of identity, provided the deceased was a resident of this state; (b) special proceedings under Sections 1170 to 1175 P.C., and the recording of the decree obtained; (c) the issuance of letters testamentary or of administration in probate proceedings upon the estate of the decedent, provided an affidavit of identity is recorded referring to those proceedings rather than to a death certificate.

If the property is registered under the Land Title Act, the fact of death must be established under Sections 1170 to 1175 P.C., or under Section 98 of the Land Title Act.

Do not overlook the fact that the lien of inheritance tax may attach to the property of the survivor. A waiver or letter from the inheritance tax office should be obtained if no tax is due—at least when proof of death is being established by the method outlined in (a).

JUDGMENTS (MONEY)

31.01 DEFINITION

A judgment is the final determination of the rights of the parties in an action or proceeding, but it is not final until the time to appeal has elapsed, or until the time has elapsed in which the party against whom a default judgment is taken may move to set it aside, or answer to the merits of the action.

31.02 LIEN

An abstract of the judgment of **any court of this state, including a judgment of any court sitting as a** small claims court, or any court of record of the United States, the enforcement of which has not been stayed on appeal, certified by the clerk or justice of the court where such judgment or decree was rendered, may be recorded with the recorder of any county and **from such recording the judgment or decree becomes a lien** upon all the real property of the judgment debtor, not exempt from execution, in such county, owned by him at the time, or which he may afterwards, and before the lien expires, acquire. (A recorded transcript or certified copy of a judgment should be considered sufficient as an abstract.)

Such lien continues for ten years from the date of entry of the judgment or decree, unless the enforcement of the judgment or decree is stayed on appeal or unless it is previously satisfied or the lien otherwise discharged. Prior to September 7, 1955, the lien period was five years.

31.03 **FINES**

A judgment in a criminal action that defendant pay a fine may be made a lien in like manner as a judgment for money in a civil action and execution may be issued thereon.

31.04 **JUDGMENT AGAINST LESSEE**

When a lease is for a definite period it is personal property, and a judgment against the lessee is not a lien thereon but an execution may be levied on the leasehold interest.

When the lease is for an indefinite period, as in the case of most oil leases, it has been held to be real property, and a judgment against the lessee in such case would appear to be a lien thereon if an abstract is recorded.

31.05 **JUDGMENT AGAINST VENDEE**—See Agreements of Sale, Section 3.02.

31.06 **AFTER ACQUIRED PROPERTY**

The creditor who first levies execution obtains a prior lien where several judgments become liens on property acquired by the debtor **after** the respective abstracts of judgment are recorded.

31.07 JUDGMENTS AGAINST ADMINISTRATORS, EXECUTORS, TRUSTEES, ETC.

Such judgments, even though abstracts are recorded, are not liens against property owned by them individually; but they are individually liable for costs (subject to reimbursement), unless by the judgment the costs are made chargeable only upon the estate. (103 Cal. 252.) Likewise a judgment against an executor or administrator is not a lien on property of the estate, but is payable in course of administration.

Judgments against heirs or devisees of a decedent, however, are liens against their interest in the estate.

31.08 ALTERNATIVE JUDGMENT

A judgment for the return of certain property or its value, as stated therein, does not create a lien except as to costs, if any.

31.09 IF JUDGMENT DEBTOR DIES

A judgment does not cease to be a lien after the death of the debtor, though an execution cannot issue. A title company will not ignore such a judgment, for it has been held that the judgment creditor may foreclose his lien by an equitable action.

31.10 DEFICIENCY JUDGMENTS

A—**Definition:** A personal judgment against any person liable for the mortgage or trust deed debt for the amount remaining due the mortgagee or beneficiary after foreclosure.

B—**Lien:** A deficiency judgment becomes a lien when an abstract thereof is recorded in the county recorder's office.

C—As to a deed of trust or mortgage **executed on or after September 19, 1939,** a deficiency judgment cannot be obtained if the real property has been sold **under the power of sale** contained therein. (580d, C.C.P.)

D—As to a **purchase price** deed of trust or mortgage executed **on or after August 21, 1933,** a deficiency judgment cannot be obtained following a sale of real property thereunder. (580b, C.C.P.)

E—Since August 21, 1933, any action for a deficiency judgment must be brought within **three months after the sale** under a deed of trust or mortgage with power of sale. (580a, C.C.P.) This limitation applies to any sale made after August 21, 1933, even though the deed of trust may be dated prior.

If a deficiency judgment is sought following a **decree of foreclosure,** the application for the hearing prior to the rendering of a deficiency judgment must be made **within three months after the foreclosure sale.** (726, C.C.P., as amended August 27, 1937.)

F—A deficiency judgment obtained following a sale under a deed of trust or mortgage with power of sale **executed on or after August 21, 1933,** or following a **decree of foreclosure** of a mortgage or **deed of trust executed on or after August 21, 1933,** may not exceed the difference between the fair value of the property at the time of sale and the total indebtedness. In no case, however, may the judgment exceed the difference between the amount of the sale and the total indebtedness. (580a and 726, C.C.P.)

G—If the debtor redeems, following a mortgage foreclosure sale or an execution sale, any deficiency judgment that has been obtained against him and recorded may at once attach as a lien. If the debtor's successor in interest redeems it does not attach.

THE LIEN OF A JUDGMENT IS TERMINATED

31.11   A—By a satisfaction of the judgment

Satisfaction of a judgment may be entered upon an execution returned satisfied, or upon an acknowledgment of satisfaction filed with the clerk or with the justice, if there be no clerk, which may recite payment of the judgment in full or the acceptance by the judgment creditor of any lesser sum in full satisfaction thereof, made in the manner of an acknowledgment of a conveyance of real property, by the judgment creditor or assignee of record, or by endorsement by judgment creditor or assignees of record on the face or on the margin of the record of the judgment, or by the attorney, unless a revocation of his authority is filed. Whenever a judgment is satisfied in fact, otherwise than upon an execution, the party or attorney must give such acknowledgment or make such endorsement and, upon motion, the court may compel it or may order the entry of satisfaction to be made without it.

Whenever an abstract of the judgment has been recorded with the recorder of any county, satisfaction thereof made in the manner of an acknowledgment of a conveyance of real property may be recorded.

One of a firm of attorneys may release a judgment.

The attorney for the creditor cannot release from the lien of the judgment a portion of the land subject thereto without express written authority from the creditor. It must be made by the creditor himself.

An **unconditional** satisfaction of judgment as to one of two or more joint debtors is a complete satisfaction of the judgment as to the party released.

A satisfaction of a judgment in favor of a minor or incompetent should be executed pursuant to the provisions of Section 372 C.C.P. The attorney is not authorized to execute the satisfaction.

31.12   **B—By an appeal taken from a money judgment and a stay bond filed.**

Upon an appeal from a Superior Court the bond must be in double the amount named in the judgment, exclusive of costs.

Upon an appeal from a Justice's or Municipal Court, the bond must be in double the amount of the judgment **inclusive** of costs. In Justice's Court appeals a hundred-dollar bond is also required to cover costs of appeal.

Upon appeals from the Municipal Court the adverse party may except to the sufficiency of the sureties within five days after service of written notice of the filing of the undertaking; and unless they or other sureties justify before a judge or the clerk of the court within five days thereafter, upon notice to the adverse party, proceedings may be had as if no undertaking had been given.

Upon appeals from the Superior Court, the adverse party may except to the sufficiency of the sureties at any time within thirty days after notice of filing such undertaking; and unless they or other sureties, within twenty days after the appellant has been served with notice of such exception, justify before a judge of the court below, upon five days' notice to respondent of the time and place of justification, execution is no longer stayed, but it is stayed up to that time, if the bond is sufficient in form.

A deposit in the court below of the amount of the judgment appealed from is equivalent to filing the undertaking.

In all cases the undertaking may be waived by the written consent of respondent.

Where the bond is sufficient in form, but the sureties, on exception, fail or refuse to justify, a second bond cannot be filed, except upon order of the higher court.

31.13   C—By granting of a new trial or the entry of an order of court setting aside the judgment.

The judgment will not be ignored by a title company, however, if an appeal is pending from the order granting a new trial or setting aside the judgment, or if the time to appeal has not elapsed.

An order setting aside a judgment is an appealable order, also an order granting a new trial. There is no right of appeal from an order denying a new trial, but the appeal must be taken from the judgment.

The effect of an appeal from an order vacating a judgment is not to restore the judgment. It no longer exists, so far as the assertion of any rights under it is concerned, until brought into force again by a reversal of the order vacating it. The code does not provide that an order appealed from shall cease to exist, but that it cannot be enforced, if stayed. Only orders that command or permit some act to be done can be stayed. An appeal from an order setting aside the satisfaction of a judgment does not restore the entry of satisfaction, nor preclude the execution of the judgment pending the appeal (at sole peril of its result) where there is no stay. (139 Cal. 140.)

31.14 TIME WHEN APPEAL MAY BE TAKEN

Appeal may be taken from any judgment of a **superior court,** from which an appeal lies, within 60 days from date of entry of the judgment—unless there has been filed a notice of motion for a new trial or a motion to vacate a judgment or to vacate and enter another and different judgment, in any of which events the time for appeal is extended in the manner provided by Rule 3 in Rules on Appeal adopted in 1943 (and amended) by the Judicial Council of the State of California.

Appeal may be taken from any judgment of a **municipal court** within 30 days after **notice** of the entry of judgment but not in any event later than 60 days from the date of entry of the judgment—unless there has been filed a notice of motion for a new trial or a motion to vacate a judgment or to vacate and enter another and different judgment, in any of which events the time for appeals is extended in the manner provided by Rule 3 of Rules on Appeal from Municipal Courts adopted in 1945 (and amended).

An appeal may be taken from a **federal court** judgment within 3 months from the entry thereof.

LEASES

32.01 IN GENERAL

A—Leases of real property for a longer period than one year should be in writing. Leases of community real property acquired on or after July 27, 1917 must be executed by both husband and wife unless for a period not exceeding one year.

B—Leases for a definite period are personal property. Those for an indefinite period—as most oil leases—have been held to be real property and will be treated by the title company as such. A lease for a definite period terminates upon its expiration date and thereafter will ordinarily be ignored by a title company, unless the records disclose a renewal.

C—**Effect of Deed**. See under topic of Deeds, General Information. Section 14.05-J.

D—**For Judgments Against Lessees**. See under topic of Judgments. Section 31.04.

E—An instrument cancelling a lease should be executed by both the lessor and lessee, or their successors in interest, or a quitclaim deed may be used, provided it appears that the same was accepted by the lessor, or his successor in interest, as cancelling the lease. **(But see Community Oil Leases.)**

F—Personal property (including leases) acquired by a married woman by an instrument in writing on or after July 29, 1927 (other than by gift, bequest, devise, descent or by deed or assignment from her husband—which is her separate property) is **presumptively her separate property.**

32.02 **COMMUNITY OIL LEASES**

A cancellation or a surrender of rights by all the lessors in a community oil lease (including counterparts), or their successors in interest, is ordinarily essential, in addition to a cancellation or quitclaim from the lessee, sub-lessee, assignee, and holders of royalty interests (both landowners' and lessees'), before any parcel or all the parcels will be clear of the lease.

The community provisions of the lease and its provisions for cancellation should be carefully examined to determine this matter.

In passing upon a purported cancellation of a community oil lease or in furnishing a report on the names of parties necessary to such a cancellation, a title company ordinarily will make a full search of all land within the community area, including parcels that the lessee has already surrendered. Reservations and recitals in deeds from lessors and their successors will be examined to determine whether or not rights under the lease passed with the deeds. Furthermore, in its search, a title company will not ordinarily ignore the rights of holders of royalty or beneficial interests, even if such rights may be personal property, and even if they are not disclosed of record.

(When **insuring** deeds or assignments conveying a series of undivided interests in oil or oil land or oil leases or deeds conveying a series of oil-bearing lots, a title company will take into consideration the question of whether or not such conveyances come within the purview of the Corporate Securities Act. See Section 12.02 herein.)

32.03   LIMITATIONS ON THE TERMS OF LEASES

See Section 842, Prob. C., for limitations on the terms of leases executed by **executors or administrators.**

See Section 717 et seq., C.C., for limitations on terms of leases of **municipal property.** (See, also, Section 7057, Publ. Res. Code, and Section 37383, Gov't Code.)

See Section 717, C.C., for limitations on terms of leases for **agricultural or horticultural purposes.**

See Section 1538.5, Prob. C., for limitation on terms of leases executed by **guardians.** Provision is made for the execution of a community oil lease by a guardian.

32.04   OIL AND GAS LEASES, FICTITIOUS

Section 1219 of the Civil Code, as amended September 7, 1955, provides for the recording of a "fictitious oil and gas lease," if it has a notation upon its face that it is fictitious. Thereafter any of its provisions may be included by reference, without setting the same forth in full, in any oil and gas lease recorded in the same county in which the fictitious oil and gas lease is recorded. The fictitious oil and gas lease need not be acknowledged, or proved, or certified, to be entitled to recordation.

LIFE ESTATES

33.01   DEFINITION AND NATURE

A life estate is an estate whose duration is limited to the life of the person holding it, or of some other person. (It embraces estates not determinable at will and held for an indefinite period, which may endure for the life or lives of persons in being, but not beyond the period of a life, such as to a man while he continues to live on the land, to a man and wife during coverture, to a woman so long as she remains unmarried, etc. See 16 Cal. Jur. 366.) It is not essential that the term "life estate" or "for life" be used.

It may be created in real or personal property, or in an estate for years.

Successive estates for life cannot be limited except to persons in being at the creation thereof, and all life estates subsequent to those of the persons in being are void. Also no estate for life can be limited as a remainder on a term of years, except to a person in being at the creation of such estate.

33.02 CREATION

A life estate may be created by a conveyance to the life tenant with remainder over; or by a reservation to the grantor; or by the irrevocable deposit of a deed in escrow to be delivered upon the death of the grantor, in which case title vests immediately in the grantee, subject to a life estate in the grantor; or by devise in a will and in the decree of distribution of the estate of the testator.

Where a deed is made to one for life, with remainder over to his heirs, or to the heirs of his body, he takes a life estate only.

A conveyance of a fee simple in the granting clause may be limited to a life estate by the habendum, or other clauses.

33.03 GENERAL INFORMATION

The life tenant is in effect the owner of the property during his life, except he must not commit waste, and he has no power to consume the principal, unless empowered. But he may be given power to sell or dispose of the fee. (See 167 Cal. 570.) Ordinarily he is entitled to the income from the property, and may make leases, or dispose of his interest, but he has no interest which he can dispose of by will, unless expressly empowered. He must pay the taxes and other annual charges and a just proportion of extraordinary assessments benefiting the whole inheritance. (840, C.C.)

A conveyance from the life tenant conveys his interest only, and the grantee's interest will terminate upon the death of the grantor. The remainderman's rights are unaffected by such conveyance unless the life tenant has power to dispose of the fee.

A conveyance by both the life tenant and the remainderman conveys the full title.

The lien of a mortgage or trust deed executed by the life tenant only, or any title acquired thereunder, terminates upon his death.

Upon the death of the life tenant, or other termination of the life estate, the full title should be shown vested in the remainderman. Such death may be established of record in the same manner as that of a joint tenant. **See Termination of Joint Tenancy By Death,** Section 30.08 under the topic of Joint Tenancy. There also may be an inheritance tax question. See 28.02.

MAPS AND SUBDIVISIONS

34.01 **WHAT IS A SUBDIVISION**

The laws governing the subdivision of real estate are contained in two different parts of the Business and Professions Code. One part, known as the "Subdivision Map Act," enables cities and counties to pass ordinances governing subdivisions, and sets forth the requirements for obtaining a subdivision map. The other part, regulating the sale of subdivided lands, and known as the California Real Estate Law, is administered by the Real Estate Commissioner.

The Subdivision Map Act defines a "subdivision" (see Section 11535, Business and Professions Code) as "any real property, improved or unimproved, or portion thereof, shown on the last preceding tax roll as a unit or as contiguous units, which is divided for the purpose of lease or for the purpose of sale, whether immediate or future, by any subdivider into five or more parcels within any one-year period."

There are two exceptions to this definition, for the term "subdivision" does not include either of the following:

"1. Any parcel or parcels of land in which all of the following conditions are present: (i) Which contain less than five acres, (ii) which abut upon public streets or highways, (iii) in which street opening or widening drainage facilities or other improvements are not required by the governing body in dividing the land into lots or parcels, and (iv) the lot design meets the approval of the governing body.

"2. Any parcel or parcels divided into lot or parcels, each of a net area of twenty acres or more, to be sold or leased for commercial agricultural purposes each of which abuts upon an improved public street or highway and has a lot design which meets the approval of the governing body."

In either of these excepted cases, it is required that a tentative map and a record of survey map be filed for record pursuant to Chapter 15, Division 3, Business and Professions Code.

The Subdivision Map Act does not apply to land dedicated for cemetery purposes.

In 1959 the following sections were added to the Business and Professions Code:

Section 11629 was added to permit the recordation of an amendment of an original map to correct an error in any course or distance or to add any omitted course or distance.

Section 11640 was added to permit the governing body of a city or county to withdraw approval of a subdivision map if no lots have been sold within 5 years or if no improvements have been made within 2 years from the date of recordation of the final map.

34.02 PERSONS REQUIRED TO SIGN FINAL SUBDIVISION MAP

On the final map must appear:
"A certificate, signed and acknowledged by all parties

having any record title interest in the land subdivided."

Signatures of parties owning the following types of interests are not required if the names of such parties and the nature of their respective interests are indorsed on the map:

A—"Rights of way, easements or other interests, none of which can ripen into a fee and which signatures are not required by the governing body."

B—"Rights of way, easements or reversions, which by reason of changed conditions, long disuse or laches appear to be no longer of practical use or value and which signatures it is impossible or impractical to obtain. In this case a reasonable statement of the circumstances preventing the procurement of such signatures shall be indorsed on the map."

C—"Interests in or rights to minerals, including but not limited to oil, gas, or other hydrocarbon substances, if (a) the ownership of such interests or rights does not include a right of entry on the surface of the land, or (b) the use of the land, or the surface thereof, in connection with the ownership of such interests or rights is prohibited by zoning or other governmental regulations of the governing body and the signatures of the owners of such interests or rights are waived by the governing body."

Beneficial interests under deeds of trust or trust interest under bond indentures and reservations in state or federal patents are not deemed to be an interest in the land within the act.

In addition to the foregoing, the map requires certificates by the engineer or surveyor and by certain public officials.

Before the county recorder will accept the map for recording, he will require evidence from the subdivider that the parties consenting to the recordation of the map are all the parties required. A **Subdivision Guarantee,** prepared by a title company, is the usual form of evidence used to meet this requirement.

34.03 TAXES AND ASSESSMENTS

Prior to the filing of the final map with the governing body, the subdivider is required to file with the clerk of the board of supervisors an official certificate that "there are no liens against the subdivision or any part thereof for unpaid state, county, municipal or local taxes or special assessments collected as taxes, except taxes or special assessments not yet payable."

An estimate of the amount of taxes and assessments which are a lien but not yet payable must also be filed with this clerk.

As to these taxes or assessments which are a lien but not yet payable, the final map cannot be recorded until the owner or subdivider executes and files with the board of supervisors a bond to be approved by the board and by its terms made to inure to the benefit of the county and conditioned upon the payment of said taxes and assessments. In lieu of a bond, a deposit of money or negotiable bonds in the same amount may be made.

34.04 TENTATIVE AND FINAL MAPS

The Subdivision Map Act provides that if the subdivider desires to record a final map, he shall comply with all its provisions, and, if there is a local ordinance, with all of its provisions. The initial action in connection with the making of any subdivision is the preparation of a tentative map or maps. Within one year after approval or conditional approval of the tentative map or maps, the subdivider may cause the subdivision, or any part thereof, to be surveyed and a final map to be prepared in accordance with the tentative map as approved. Upon application of the subdivider an extension of not exceeding one year may be granted. Any failure to record a final map within one year from the approval or conditional approval of the tentative map or any extension thereof shall terminate all proceedings. Before a final map may thereafter be recorded, a new tentative map must be submitted.

Effective September 7, 1955, references to "record of survey" were deleted from the Subdivision Map

Act, as well as provisions that a subdivider may elect to use a record of survey map rather than a final map. (Record of survey maps may still be used, however, as to property not within the meaning of "subdivision" as defined in Section 11535 of said Code, but there is no longer a requirement that they contain the data and information called for by the sections amended or repealed. (See definition in Section 34.01.) **Conveyances of any part of a subdivision shall not be made by lot or block number, initial or other designation, unless and until final map has been recorded.**

Section 11612.5 was added to the Business and Professions Code in 1959 to provide a procedure whereby any city or county may, by ordinance, provide that a subdivider may elect to install improvements in only a portion of a subdivision, and to deposit in escrow a deed to the balance of the subdivision with escrow instructions which would instruct the escrow title holder to reconvey to the subdivider from time to time, on approval of the governing body, the remaining portions of the property.

34.05 UNLAWFUL SALES

It is unlawful to offer to sell or lease, to contract to sell or lease, or to sell or lease any subdivision or any part thereof until a **final map** thereof, in full compliance with the provisions of the Subdivision Map Act and of any local ordinance, has been duly recorded or filed in the office of the county recorder.

This does not apply, however, to any parcel or parcels of a subdivision offered for sale or lease, contracted for sale or lease, or sold or leased, in compliance with or exempt from any law (including a local ordinance) regulating the design and improvement of subdivisions in effect at the time the subdivision was established.

34.06 DEED OR SALE BY MAP THAT DOES NOT MEET LEGAL REQUIREMENTS

Any deed of conveyance, sale or contract to sell made contrary to the provisions of the Subdivision

Map Act is voidable at the sole option of the grantee, buyer or person contracting to purchase, within one year after the date of execution of the deed, sale or contract of sale.

34.07 CONVEYANCES PRIOR TO RECORDING OF FINAL MAP

Conveyances of any part of a subdivision shall not be made by lot or block number, initial or other designation, unless and until a final map has been recorded.

34.08 REGULATING SALES OF SUBDIVIDED LANDS

Regulation of the sale of subdivided lands is covered by the Business and Professions Code. See Sections 11000 et seq. "Subdivided lands" and "subdivisions," as defined in Section 11000, refer to "improved or unimproved land or lands divided or proposed to be divided for the purpose of sale or lease or financing, whether immediate or future, into 5 or more lots or parcels; provided, however, that land or lands sold by lots or parcels of not less than 160 acres which are designated by such lot or parcel description by government surveys and appear as such on the current assessment roll of the county in which such land or lands are situated shall not be deemed to be subdivided lands or a subdivision within the meaning of this section, unless such land or lands are divided or proposed to be divided for the purpose of sale for oil and gas purposes."

The act does not apply to the leasing of apartments, offices, stores, or similar space within an apartment building, industrial building, or commercial building except the leasing of apartments in a community apartment project.

Section 11000.5 of the Business and Professions Code, added September 7, 1955, excepts from the definition of a subdivision lands sold or leased solely for "commercial agricultural purposes" in parcels of 2 acres or more.

Section 11013 of said Code, as amended September 7, 1955, defines "blanket encumbrance," and Section

11013.1 to 11013.5, inclusive, added to said Code on September 7, 1955, establish the procedure to be followed with respect to subdivided lands when the subject is, and when it is not, subject to a "blanket encumbrance."

Section 11000 of said Code, amended September 7, 1955, and Section 11004, added September 7, 1955, to said Code, provide that a community apartment project in which an undivided interest in land is coupled with the right to exclusive occupancy of any apartment located thereon is subject to provisions and regulations of this part of the Code.

Prior to the time when subdivided lands are to be offered for sale or lease, the owner, his agent or subdivider must notify the real estate commissioner in writing of his intention to sell such offering—which notice of intention shall contain the information required by Section 11010.

The commissioner must make a public report of his findings, following his examination of a subdivision, and he has power to prohibit the sale or lease of property if it would constitute misrepresentation to or deceit or fraud of the purchasers of lots or parcels in the subdivisions.

4.09 **CURATIVE ACT**

As to maps or plats filed prior to April 1, 1953, this act cures any defects, omissions or informalities in the preparation or execution of such maps or of the affidavits, certificates, acknowledgments, acceptances of dedications or other required matters. It also validates all sales and conveyances of land by reference to such maps. (The ownership of the tract, or of any part of it, is not affected by the curative act, nor is the failure of necessary parties to sign the map if they still have an interest in the property subdivided, nor is any defect in measurement, surveying, or drafting.)

A method for *altering* or *vacating* a recorded map, with court approval, was provided on September 9, 1953, through the addition of Sections 11700 to 11709, Business and Professions Code, as amended in 1961.

34.10 **DEDICATION BY ADMINISTRATORS, EXECUTORS
GUARDIANS AND CONSERVATORS**

An administrator, executor, guardian or conservato
may dedicate or convey an easement to the state or t
any county or municipal corporation, or to any dis
trict or to any person, firm, association or public o
private corporation, provided it is for the best interest
of the estate and pursuant to proper order of court
(587 and 1515, Prob. C.)

34.11 **"OFFICIAL MAP" OF A CITY, TOWN OR SUB
DIVISION**

Whenever any city, town or subdivision of land i
platted or divided into lots or blocks, and wheneve
any addition to any city, town or subdivision is lai
out into lots or blocks for the purpose of sale or trans
fer, the city engineer or the county surveyor, unde
the direction and with the approval of the city counci
or board of supervisors, may make an official map o
the city, town or subdivision, giving to each block or
the map a number, and to each lot or subdivision ir
the block a separate number or letter, and giving name
to such streets, avenues, lanes, courts, commons o
parks, as may be delineated on the official map.

The engineer or surveyor, under the direction and
with the approval of the city council or board o
supervisors, may compile the map from maps on file
or may resurvey or renumber the blocks, or renumbe
or reletter the lots in the blocks, or change the name
of streets.

The map when duly certified must be filed in th
office of the county recorder. The map becomes ar
"official map when certified, filed and bound not no
before."

Whenever the city council or board of supervisor
adopts a map prepared as the official map of the sub
division, town, city or county, it shall be lawful and
sufficient to describe the lots or blocks in any deeds
conveyances, contracts, or obligations affecting any or
the lots or blocks as designated on the official map, a
reference sufficient for the identification of the map
being coupled with the description.

MEASUREMENTS

35.01 LAND MEASURE—SQUARE

144 sq. in. equals	1 sq. ft.
9 sq. ft.	1 sq. yd.
30¼ sq. yds.	1 sq. rod
16 sq. rods	1 sq. chain
40 sq. rods	1 sq. rood
1210 sq. yds.	1 sq. rood
4 roods	1 acre
1 sq. rod	272¼ sq. ft.
1 sq. chain	4356 sq. ft.
10 sq. chains	1 acre
160 sq. rods	1 acre
4840 sq. yds.	1 acre
43,560 sq. ft.	1 acre
640 acres	1 sq. mile
1 sq. mile	1 section
36 sq. miles	1 township
6 miles square	1 township

35.02 LAND MEASURE—LINEAR

7.92 inches equals	1 link
25 links	16½ ft.
25 links	1 rod
16½ ft.	1 rod
4 rods	100 links
100 links	66 ft.
100 links	1 chain
66 ft.	1 chain
1 pole	1 rod
4 poles	1 chain
10 chains	1 furlong
80 chains	1 mile
320 rods	1 mile
8000 links	1 mile
5280 ft.	1 mile
1760 yds.	1 mile
1 league	3 miles
1 league (Spanish)	2⅗ miles
1 vara	33 inches
1 vara	2¾ ft.

35.03 AN ACRE IS

43,560 square feet
165 feet by 264 feet
198 feet by 220 feet
660 feet by 66 feet
160 square rods
208 ft. 8½ in. square

35.04 BEARING

If no mention is made that the bearing is magnetic it is understood to be true.

The magnetic declination in Los Angeles County was about 14½ degrees East at time when most maps using magnetic bearings were made.

To change magnetic bearing to true bearing, add the declination if bearing is either N.E. or S.W. and subtract if it is N.W. or S.E.

35.05 CURVES, CIRCLES, ETC.

The degree of a curve is determined by the central angle which is subtended by a chord of 100 feet.

The deflection angle of a curve is the angle formed at any point of same between a tangent and a chord of 100 feet and is half the degree of a curve.

The radius of a 1 degree curve is 5729.65 feet or 5730 feet for practical use. The radius of any curve can be found by dividing this number by the number of degrees of a curve.

To read the length of a course between stations as marked by surveying, subtract the lower from the higher: 12 plus 52 from 17 plus 83 is 5 plus 31, equal to 531 feet.

Circumference circle is diameter times 3.1416.

Length of arc is number of degrees times .017453 radius.

Area circle is diam. sq. times .7854.

MECHANICS' LIENS
(Also see "Building Contracts")

36.01 DEFINITION

A lien is a charge imposed upon specific property by which said property is made security for the performance of an act.

A mechanics' lien is a lien upon property accorded by the constitution of the State of California and statutes enacted pursuant thereto, to secure the compensation of those who, pursuant to contract, have been directly instrumental in its improvement.

36.02 BY WHOM MECHANICS' LIENS MAY BE FILED

Mechanics, materialmen, contractors, subcontractors, artisans, architects, machinists, builders, teamsters, and draymen, and all persons and laborers of every class performing labor upon, or bestowing skill or other necessary services on, or furnishing materials to be used or consumed in, or furnishing appliances, teams or power contributing to, the construction, alteration, addition to, or repair, either in whole or in part, of any building, structure, or other work of improvement shall have a lien upon the property upon which they have bestowed labor or furnished materials or appliances for the value of the use of such labor done or materials furnished and for the value of the use of such appliances, teams, or power, whether done or furnished at the instance of the owner or of any other person acting by his authority or under him, as contractor or otherwise.

36.03 WHEN LIENS MAY BE FILED

A—By the original contractor within 60 days after the completion of his contract and after the filing for record of the notice of completion.

B—By any claimant other than the original contractor after he has ceased to perform labor or furnish materials, or both, and within 30 days after the filing for record of the notice of completion.

C—But in case a valid notice of completion is not recorded, then all persons have ninety days after the completion of said work of improvement within which to file liens.

Section 1193 was added to the Code of Civil Procedure in 1959 to require that the person claiming a lien, except claimants under direct contract with the owner or performing labor for wages, must give written notice to the owner and general contractor at least 15 days prior to the filing of the lien.

36.04 RESIDENTIAL UNITS

Section 1182 of the Code of Civil Procedure defines the phrase "work of improvement" and the word "improvement" as "the entire structure or scheme of improvement as a whole." But Section 1194.1, effective September 22, 1951, provides that where "a work of improvement consists in the construction of two or more separate residential units, each such unit shall be considered a separate 'work of improvement' or 'improvement', and the time for filing claims of lien against each such residential unit as provided in this chapter shall commence to run upon the completion of each such residential unit. A separate residential unit is defined as consisting of one residential structure together with any garages or other outbuildings appurtenant thereto. The provisions of this proviso shall not impair any rights conferred under the provisions of Sections 1192.1, 1194.1, and 1184.1 of this code. Materials delivered to or upon any portion of said entire work of improvement and ultimately used or consumed in one of such separate residential units shall, for all the purposes of this chapter, be deemed to have been furnished to be used or consumed in the separate residential unit in which the same shall have been actually used or consumed; provided, however, that if the lien claimant is unable to segregate the amounts used on or consumed in such separate residential units he shall be entitled to all the benefits of Section 1194.1 of this code."

36.05 RECORD AND PRIORITY

The claim of lien must be filed in the recorder's office of the county in which the property or some part thereof is situated, and thereupon has priority over any lien, mortgage, deed of trust, or other encumbrance which may have attached subsequent to the time when the building or work of improvement was **commenced**; also to any lien, mortgage, deed of trust, or other encumbrance of which the lien claimant had no notice and which was unrecorded at the time the building or work of improvement was **commenced**.

The holder of any mortgage or deed of trust who procures a bond with sufficient sureties (complying with Section 1188.2 C.C.P.) and files the bond in the recorder's office gains priority over liens for work done or materials furnished after the date the bond is filed.

36.06 EVIDENCE OF COMMENCEMENT OF WORK

Title companies, when called upon to insure the priority of the lien of a deed of trust or mortgage over possible claims under mechanics' liens, will inspect the property in question just prior to recordation of the deed of trust or mortgage. Discovery of any of the following is usually considered evidence that work has already been commenced:

A—**Building materials or equipment deposited**, whether on the property in question or on an adjoining property, if designed for use on the first mentioned.

B—**Foundation stakes** set by surveyor. (This does not refer to land boundary stakes.)

C—**Test holes dug.**

D—**Load of dirt deposited.**

E—**Trees, shrubs and weeds removed.**

F—**Water meter set in parking place by contractor.**

G—**Preliminary landscaping.**

H—**Installation of sprinkling system.**

I—**Demolition of old buildings, retaining walls, or fences.**

36.07 LIEN ON LOTS FOR GRADING OR IMPROVEMENT OF ADJOINING STREETS

Any person who, at the instance or request of the owner (or any other person acting by his authority or under him, as contractor or otherwise) of any lot or tract of land, grades, fills in, or otherwise improves the same, or the street, highway, or sidewalk in front of or adjoining the same, or constructs or installs sewers or other public utilities therein, or constructs any areas, or vaults, or cellars, or rooms, under said sidewalks, or makes any improvements in connection therewith, has a lien upon said lot or tract of land for his work done and materials furnished. (Section 1184.1, added September 22, 1951 to the Code of Civil Procedure.)

If such work of improvement is provided for in a separate contract from any contract for the erection of residential units or other structures upon said lot or tract of land, then the work of improvement is a separate work of improvement and its commencement is not a commencement of work on the lot or tract of land. All as provided in Section 1189.1, added September 22, 1951 to the Code of Civil Procedure, which goes on to explain the circumstances under which liens for such work are prior to mortgages, deeds of trust or other encumbrances.

36.08 **WHO IS AN ORIGINAL CONTRACTOR**

A—In General. One who contracts directly with the owner, or his agent, to do the work and furnish the materials (a) for the whole of the work of construction; or (b) for a particular portion of such work. Thus the owner may enter into different original contracts, such as for plumbing, painting or papering, the test being whether there may be intermediate lien holders in each case.

B—Laborers and Materialmen. A materialman, as such, is not an original contractor, and one who sells material to him, or is employed by him, is not entitled to a lien, since one who furnishes material or performs labor directly for the owner is not an original contractor. Hence his claim of lien must be filed within thirty days, if a notice of completion or cessation is recorded.

36.09 **WHAT IS "COMPLETION"**

Section 1193.1, added on September 22, 1951 to the Code of Civil Procedure, provides that any of the following shall be deemed equivalent to a completion:

A—The occupation or use of a work of improvement by the owner, or his agent, accompanied by cessation from labor thereon;

B—The acceptance by the owner, or his agent, of the work of improvement; or

C—After the commencement of a work of improvement, a cessation of labor thereon for a continuous period of 60 days, or a cessation of labor thereon for a continuous period of 30 days or more if the owner files for record a valid notice of cessation.

If the work of improvement is of the character referred to in Section 1184.1 of said Code (See Section 36.07, Handbook) and is subject to acceptance by any public or governmental authority, the completion of such work of improvement is the date of such acceptance.

36.10A NOTICE OF COMPLETION

A notice of completion (signed and verified by the owner or his agent) must be filed in the office of the county recorder of the county in which the property is situated.

It must be filed **within ten days** after the completion of the work of improvement provided for in the original contract or, if there are two or more original contracts, after the completion of any one contract for a particular portion of the work of improvement. (The original contractor then has 60 days, and every other claimant 30 days, after the filing of this notice to file for record his claim of lien.)

This notice of completion must set forth:

(1) The date of completion of the work of improvement or of the particular portion of the work of improvement. (It is not invalidated, however, if it recites an erroneous date of completion provided the true date is within 10 days preceding the date of filing for record of the notice.)

(2) The name and address of such owner. If there are co-owners and the notice is signed by less than all such co-owners, their names and addresses must

be recited. The word "owner" means the one who caused the building to be constructed (or his successor in interest), whether the owner's interest is in fee, as vendee, as lessee, or other interest.

Section 1193.1 of the Code of Civil Procedure was amended in 1959 to provide that any notice of completion signed by a successor in interest of an owner shall recite the names and addresses of his transferor or transferors.

(3) The nature of the interest or estate of such owner.

(4) A description of the property sufficient for identification, including street address if one has been given. (If a sufficient legal description is given, the validity of the notice is not affected by an erroneous street address or the omission of one.)

(5) The name of the original contractor for the work of improvement, or, if the notice is given only of completion of a contract for a particular portion, then the name of the original contractor under such contract and a general statement of the kind of work done or materials furnished pursuant to such contract.

A valid notice of completion can be ignored by a title company 60 days after the recording date. If the notice is defective, it can be ignored 90 days after the date of actual completion.

36.10B **NOTICE OF CESSATION**

A notice of cessation (signed and verified by the owner or his agent) must be filed in the office of the county recorder of the county in which the property is situated.

If, after the commencement of a work of improvement, there shall be a cessation of labor thereon for a continuous period of 60 days, then all claimants have **90 days from the expiration of such 60-day period** within which to file for record their claims of lien; **provided,** that if, after there shall be a cessation of labor thereon for a **continuous period of 30 days or**

more, the owner files for record a valid notice of cessation, every original contractor has 60 days, and every other claimant 30 days, within which to file for record his claim of lien.

This notice of cessation must set forth:

(1) The date on or about when the cessation from labor occurred.

(2) A statement that such cessation continued until the giving of such notice of cessation.

(3) The name and address of the owner. (The word "owner" is used in the same sense as in connection with a notice of completion. See Section 36.10A)

(4) The nature of the interest or estate of such owner.

(5) A description of the property sufficient for identification. (See Section 36.10A)

(6) The name of the original contractor, if any, for the work of improvement as a whole.

A valid notice of cessation can be ignored by a title company 60 days after the recording date. If the notice is defective, or if no notice has been filed, the facts about actual cessation will govern. If there has been a cessation of labor for a continuous period of 60 days and no notice of cessation has been filed, all claimants have 90 days from the expiration of the 60-day period within which to file for record their claims of lien.

36.11 HOW LONG DOES A LIEN BIND PROPERTY

A mechanic's lien binds property for ninety days from the date of recording the claim of the lien or for ninety days after the expiration of credit given (notice of the facts and terms of such credit having been filed in the county recorder's office within the ninety-day period following the filing of the lien)—unless the lien is sooner released. If an action to foreclose is commenced within the ninety-day (or extended) period the lien continues.

Extension can be for a period not longer than one

year from completion of the work by any agreement to give credit.

If foreclosure proceedings are not prosecuted to trial within two years after the commencement thereof, the court may in its discretion dismiss the same for want of prosecution.

A title company will not automatically ignore a mechanic's lien 90 days after it has been recorded or 90 days after the elapse of the extension or credit period, even if no action to foreclose the lien is pending. Bankruptcy proceedings against the record owner might extend the period for foreclosure. Furthermore, since the 90-day provision of the code has been construed as a statute of **limitations,** disability, absence from the state, military service, and other facts, including an **off-record** extension, might operate to bar the statute. Circumstances will determine when a mechanic's lien may be ignored.

Section 1193.2 was added to the Code of Civil Procedure in 1957 authorizing the recording of a bond by the owner of property sought to be charged with a mechanic's lien where the owner disputes the correctness or validity of the alleged lien, which bond shall be in a penal sum equal to 1½ times the amount of the claim, or if such claim of lien affects more than 1 parcel of real property, then 1½ times the amount allocated to the parcel or parcels in the claim of lien. Upon the recording of a sufficient bond, the real property described in the bond is freed from the claim of lien and any action brought to foreclose the lien. In 1959 the Section was amended to allow, in addition to an owner, the contractor or subcontractor to file a bond to release a mechanic's lien.

36.12 **NOTICE OF NON-RESPONSIBILITY**

A—The owner or any person having or claiming any estate in the land may, **within ten days after obtaining knowledge of construction,** give notice that he will not be responsible for the same by posting a notice on the property and recording a verified copy thereof, said notice to contain a description of the property, with name and nature of title or interest of person giving same, name of purchaser under contract, if any, or lessee, if known. If such notice is not given, the improvement will be held to have been constructed at the instance of such owner or other person, if he had knowledge thereof, and such interest owned or claimed will be subject to any lien that may be filed.

B—A title company will ignore a notice of non-responsibility in a policy if a notice of **completion** of the construction work referred to has been filed and the lien period has expired. It is the possibility of future mechanics' liens arising from facts disclosed by the notice that concerns a title company rather than the notice itself.

If no notice of completion has been filed, a title company ordinarily will ignore a notice of non-responsibility that has been of record two years. (If construction work were extended over a long period, as in the case of a large building, it might not be safe to ignore the notice that soon.) Inspection of the premises or information outside the records sometimes takes the place, for the purposes of a title insurance company, of the notice of completion.

C—The validity of a notice of non-responsibility cannot be determined from the records since they will not disclose whether compliance has been made with the code requirements as to time or posting on the premises. If such posting has not been made, the recorded notice affords no protection from mechanics' liens.

36.13 MECHANICS' LIENS CANNOT BE IGNORED AFTER FORECLOSURE OF TRUST DEED

Mechanics' liens that are alive will not be ignored by a title company even though they are filed after the recording of the trust deed later foreclosed and even though they contain recitals that the work was done and the materials furnished after such recording date. A suit to quiet title is often necessary to eliminate these liens.

36.14 REASONS WHY MECHANICS' LIENS CANNOT BE IGNORED AFTER FORECLOSURE OF TRUST DEED

All mechanics' liens relate back to the **time of commencement** of the building, improvements, structure or work of improvement as a whole.

(This is true regardless of whether or not there was a general contract and regardless of recitals as to the date of starting work contained in a particular claim of lien.)

If the time of commencement of the building, improvement, structure or work of improvement is prior to the recording of the trust deed—or even prior to the **delivery** to the lender of the trust deed note—all claims of mechanics' liens are also prior to the trust deed. They are also prior, it has been held, if commencement is prior to trustor's acquisition.

36.15 TRUST DEED OR MORTGAGE RECORDED AFTER WORK COMMENCED, HOW TO GAIN PRIORITY OVER MECHANICS' LIENS ARISING OUT OF REMAINING WORK

If the holder of any mortgage or deed of trust shall procure or cause to be procured a bond complying with the provisions of Section 1188.2, CCP, and files such bond in the office of the county recorder, either concurrently with or after the recordation of such mortgage or deed of trust, then such mortgage or deed of trust shall be prior and paramount to mechanics' liens arising out of any work of improvement on said land done or materials furnished subsequent to the time such bond is filed.

MISSING PERSONS

36.01 The administration of the estates of persons missing seven years is provided for in Sections 280 to 294, inclusive, Probate Code.

MORATORIUM IN FAVOR OF PERSONS CALLED INTO MILITARY SERVICE

38.01 EFFECTIVE DATE OF RELIEF ACT

The "Soldiers' and Sailors' Civil Relief Act of 1940" became effective October 17, 1940. It was amended October 6, 1942.

38.02 DEFAULT JUDGMENTS

The Act provides that no default judgment may be entered against any person unless either an affidavit is filed by the plaintiff in the proceedings setting forth facts showing that the defendant is not in the military service or the court makes an order—after appointing an attorney to represent the defendant—directing the entry of such judgment. Unless these requirements have been met, a title company will not insure a title based upon a default entered after August 27, 1940 (effective date of the superseded National Guard Act.)

38.03 MORTGAGE OR TRUST DEED FORECLOSURES

The Act originally applied only to "obligations" originating prior to October 17, 1940, but, by the amendments of 1942, it was made applicable to all obligations originating prior to entry of the owner of the property into military service. No sale under deeds of trust or mortgages with power of sale securing such obligations shall be valid if made while the owner is in military service or if made within three months after such service terminates.

Before insuring a foreclosure sale, a title company will call for satisfactory evidence that the owner was not in military service at the time of the sale, or, if he has been in the service, that such service had terminated more than three months prior to the sale. An exception is the case of a sale authorized by order of the Superior Court, with the sale reported to the court and an order made approving it.

MORTGAGES

(Also see Bond Issues by Corporations; Foreclosure of
Mortgages; Deficiency Judgments; Foreign Administrators, etc.; Subordination Agreements; Corporate Securities Act; Chattel and Crop Mortgages; Trust
Deeds.)

41.01 DEFINITION

A mortgage is a contract by which specific property
is hypothecated for the performance of an act, without
the necessity of a change of possession. (**Distinction
between Mortgage and Trust Deed**—see Section 58.02
under topic of Trust Deeds.)

41.02 IMPORTANT FACTS ABOUT MORTGAGES

A—A mortgage may by its terms cover **after acquired property** of the mortgagor. (But if said mortgage is recorded before the mortgagor acquires title,
its recordation will not constitute constructive notice
to innocent purchasers dealing with the mortgagor,
after acquisition of title, in good faith, for value, and
without actual notice of such mortgage.)

B—A **guardian, administrator or executor** may execute, extend or assign a mortgage or deed of trust only
upon obtaining a proper order of court, and such
mortgage or assignment should contain a recital of the
authority.

He may execute a full release or cause a full reconveyance to be made without order of court.

If the mortgage or deed of trust contains a provision
for partial releases or partial reconveyances he may
likewise execute or cause to be executed such releases
or reconveyances without order of court.

On September 19, 1939, the court was given power
to authorize an executor or administrator to give a partial satisfaction of a mortgage or to cause the execution
of a partial reconveyance of a deed of trust. (Section
718.7, Probate Code.) If the decedent died prior to
September 19, 1939, it is doubtful if this section would
be applicable.

C—A mortgage or deed of trust providing for **future optional advances** creates a superior lien for the same against subsequent encumbrancers, until the holder of such mortgage or deed of trust has **actual** notice of the junior encumbrance. If future advances are made **obligatory** upon the mortgagee or beneficiary by the provisions of the mortgage or deed of trust, the lien of the mortgage or deed of trust is superior to the liens of subsequent encumbrancers which are prior to the making of such future advances.

D—The **legal rate of interest** is seven per cent per annum, but the parties to a mortgage may by express terms agree to pay not exceeding ten per cent per annum (with certain exceptions, as to which see topic of USURY, Section 61.01 et seq.).

E—The mortgage note may be dated prior or subsequent to the mortgage.

F—The **assignment of the debt** secured by a mortgage carries with it the security. An assignment may be recorded, recordation operating as constructive notice of the contents of the assignment.

G—A note and mortgage should not be drawn in favor of **"The Estate of"** a deceased person, minor or incompetent. Instead, it should be in favor of "A, as executor of the estate of John Doe, deceased" or in favor of "John Smith, a minor," or "John Smith, an incompetent." It should not ordinarily be drawn in favor of the guardian or conservator.

H—Personal property (including mortgages) acquired by a married woman by an instrument in writing on or after July 29, 1927 (other than by gift, bequest, devise, descent, or by assignment from her husband—which is her separate property) is **presumptively her separate property.** If the property is acquired on or after September 15, 1935, however, by **husband and wife,** by an instrument in which they are described as husband and wife, the presumption is that such property is the community property of said husband and wife, unless a different intention is expressed in the instrument.

I—For mortgages given to secure a bonded indebtedness, see topic of BOND ISSUES, Section 7.01 et seq.

J—**Fictitious mortgages** and **deeds of trust** of real property may be recorded with the county recorder, as provided in Section 2952, Civil Code, in effect September 19, 1947. They need not be acknowledged, but they must bear a notation on the face that they are fictitious. After recording, any of the provisions may be included **by reference** in any mortgage or deed of trust affecting real property in the same county.

41.03 **PURCHASE MONEY MORTGAGES AND DEEDS OF TRUST**

Under Section 2898 of the Civil Code, a mortgage or deed of trust given for the price of real property, at the time of its conveyance, has priority over all other liens created against the purchaser, **subject to the operation of the recording laws.** Thus it has priority over a **prior judgment** against the purchaser.

The **right of third persons** to have their mortgages upheld as purchase price mortgages is recognized only when it appears that the money was loaned to the purchaser **for the sole and express purpose and was used for the express purpose** of paying for the property. (120 Cal. 684.)

41.04 **OUTLAWED MORTGAGES** (Also see **Extensions**)

The statute of limitations may be pleaded as a bar to an action to foreclose which is commenced four years after the date of maturity of the mortgage note. This period, however, may be extended by payment on account, or by an agreement in writing executed by all parties in interest. Subsequent encumbrancers or lienors are not affected unless they join in or consent thereto.

41.05 **EXTENSIONS** (Also see **Outlawed Mortgages**)

The date of maturity of a mortgage or trust deed note may be extended by an agreement in writing executed by all parties in interest. At least in the case of a mortgage, however, junior encumbrancers or lienors are unaffected by an extension beyond the four-year period after the original date of maturity, unless they join therein or consent thereto or unless the extension is prior.

If the interest rate has been increased in an instrument extending a mortgage or trust deed, the change makes a new contract but (at least in the case of a mortgage) does not affect junior encumbrancers or lienors unless they consent thereto.

41.06 MERGER WITH FEE

If the property is conveyed to the mortgagee no merger is presumed. If a merger is intended, a release of the mortgage should be recorded.

41.07 WHEN WIFE SHOULD JOIN IN MORTGAGE ON HUSBAND'S PROPERTY

The wife must join with her husband in the execution of a mortgage or trust deed on community property, if the property was acquired subsequent to July 27, 1917.

Community property standing in the name of the husband and acquired prior to July 27, 1917, may be mortgaged by him without his wife joining in the execution thereof. (See Section 10.06.)

41.08 MORTGAGING PROPERTY OF MINORS AND INCOMPETENTS

The property of minors and incompetents cannot be encumbered except upon proper order of court.

41.09 MORTGAGES BY RELIGIOUS, SOCIAL OR BENEVOLENT CORPORATIONS

(See Sections 11.12 and 11.13.)

41.10 WHEN A MORTGAGOR OR TRUSTOR COMES BACK INTO TITLE FOLLOWING A FORECLOSURE

If a mortgagor or trustor in a **foreclosed** mortgage or deed of trust later re-acquires the title to the land, encumbrances made or suffered by him subsequent to that mortgage or deed of trust may be revived.

If the mortgagor or trustor in a **junior** mortgage or deed of trust, the lien of which was extinguished by the foreclosure of a **senior** mortgage or deed of trust, re-acquires title, the junior mortgage or deed of trust may be revived, as well as encumbrances made or suffered by said junior mortgagor or trustor that are subsequent to the junior mortgage or deed of trust.

Any grant deed executed prior to, during or after foreclosure by either of the mortgagors or trustors in the foregoing cases will be carefully examined by a title company. It might carry after-acquired title.

41.11 **ASSUMPTION OF INDEBTEDNESS BY PURCHASER**

Sections 1973 C. C. P. and 1624 C. C., listing the agreements that are invalid unless they, or some note or memorandum thereof, are in writing, were amended August 27, 1937, to include:

"An agreement by a purchaser of real property to pay an indebtedness secured by a mortgage or deed of trust upon the property purchased, unless assumption of said indebtedness by the purchaser is specifically provided for in the conveyance of such property."

41.12 **WAIVER BY BORROWER OF HIS RIGHTS**

A contemporaneous agreement by a borrower to waive certain of his legal rights and privileges with respect to a debt secured by a deed of trust, mortgage or other instrument creating a lien on real property is void. (Section 2953, C.C., in effect August 27, 1937, amended September 19, 1939, September 13, 1941.)

41.13 **DEFICIENCY JUDGMENTS**

See Section 31.10.

NAME, CHANGE OF

42.01 Section 1096 of the Civil Code provides, in part, that:

"Any person in whom the title of real estate is vested, who shall afterwards, from any cause, have his or her name changed, must, in any conveyance of said real estate so held, set forth the name in which he or she derived title to said real estate. Any conveyance, though recorded as provided by law, which does not comply with the foregoing provision shall not impart constructive notice of the contents thereof to subsequent purchasers and encumbrancers, but such conveyance is valid as between the parties thereto and those who have notice thereof."

Said Section 1096 applies also to corporations.

42.02 On and after August 14, 1929, a corporation may change its name by amendment of its articles. Prior thereto a court proceeding was necessary.

42.03 Section 751a, C.C.P., provides a method by which a subsequent owner, or successor in interest, of property conveyed by a party using a name other than that by which he acquired may petition the court to obtain an adjudication of identity of that party.

OLD AGE SECURITY LAW

43.01 By Constitutional amendment effective November 5, 1940, all liens, mortgages, encumbrances, and agreements not to convey or encumber property contained in the Old Age Security Act of 1929 (Chapter 530, Statutes of 1929) and in the Old Age Security Law (Chapter 1 of Division III of the Welfare and Institutions Code) were released and rescinded. All such may be ignored.

This does not apply to so-called **"indigent mortgages"** acquired by boards of supervisors in some counties from recipients of indigent aid granted pursuant to Chapter 761, Statutes of 1933, or pursuant to Sections 2601 to 2610, inclusive, of the Welfare and Institutions Code. These "indigent mortgages" usually contain a power of sale and usually designate a specific amount, which has at the time been advanced, and provide for the security of other amounts which may be thereafter advanced. They also usually describe a particular property and, by appropriate language, include all other property then owned or thereafter acquired by the mortgagor. When authorized by resolution of the board of supervisors, the county's lien may be released, or it may be subordinated to the lien of any mortgage or deed of trust given to renew or refinance any mortgage or deed of trust or other encumbrance the lien or charge of which had priority over the county's lien.

PARTNERSHIP

44.01 UNIFORM GENERAL AND LIMITED PARTNERSHIP LAWS

Were adopted in this state and have been in effect since August 14, 1929.

44.02 PARTNERSHIP DEFINED

A partnership is an association of two or more persons to carry on as co-owners a business for profit. A limited partnership is a partnership formed by two or more persons under the provisions of Section 15502, of the Corporations Code, having as members one or more general partners and one or more limited partners—the latter as such not to be bound by the obligation of the partnership.

(A joint adventure, sometimes called joint venture, is "a joint association of persons in a common enterprise for profit, but falling short of a partnership.")

44.03 FORMATION OF PARTNERSHIP

Every partnership transacting business in California under a fictitious name, or a designation not showing the names (surnames sufficient) of the partners, must file with the county clerk a certificate stating the names and residences of the partners, which certificate must also be published as required. (Section 2466, C.C.) The only penalty, however, for failing to file such certificate or make such publication is inability to maintain an action. A title company will not require that such certificate be filed. (See Section 44.07.)

Prior to 1959, if the partnership was a limited partnership the certificate was to be in duplicate, setting out all the information required by Section 15502, Corporations Code, and was to be filed one in the county clerk's office and the other in the county recorder's office. In 1959, Section 15502 of the Corporations Code was amended to require only one certificate, instead of duplicate certificates, and to delete the former requirement that a copy be filed with the county clerk.

A title company will not insure title in a **limited** partnership or grantee thereof until such certificate has been recorded, because a limited partnership is not lawfully formed until this has been done.

44.04   PARTNERSHIP PROPERTY

Is defined to be: (1) All property originally brought into the partnership stock or subsequently acquired by purchase or otherwise, on account of the partnership; (2) Unless the contrary intention appears, property acquired with partnership funds.

Any estate in real property may be **acquired in the partnership name** and title so acquired can be conveyed only in the partnership name. A conveyance to a partnership in the partnership name, though without words of inheritance, passes the entire estate of the grantor, unless a contrary intent appears.

Section 684 of the Civil Code provides that a partnership interest is one owned by several persons, in partnership, for partnership purposes.

44.05   AUTHORITY OF GENERAL PARTNER

Section 15009, Corporations Code, provides that every partner is an agent of the partnership for the purpose of its business, and the act of every partner, including the execution in the partnership name of any instrument, for apparently carrying on in the usual way the business of the partnership, binds the partnership, unless he has in fact no authority to act for the partnership in the particular matter, and the person with whom he is dealing has knowledge of that fact.

44.06 **CONVEYANCE OF PARTNERSHIP PROPERTY**

Where title to real property is in the partnership name, a general partner can convey title to such property by a conveyance executed in the partnership name.

However, the partnership may recover such property unless the partner's act binds the partnership under the provisions of paragraph (1) of Section 15009, Corporations Code (see Section 44.05 of this topic), or unless such property has been conveyed to a bona fide purchaser for value without knowledge that the partner, in making the conveyance, has exceeded his authority. Where the title to real property is in the names of all the partners, a conveyance executed by all the partners passes all their rights in such property. A conveyance of partnership property executed by a partner in his own name passes the equitable interest of the partnership, provided the act is one within the authority of the partner.

44.07 **WHEN PARTNERSHIP STATEMENT IS FILED IN RECORDER'S OFFICE**

Any partnership may file for record in the office of the county recorder of any county a statement of partnership, as provided in Section 15010.5, Corporations Code, whereupon it shall be presumed, in favor of any bona fide purchaser for value of partnership real property, that the persons named as partners are all the members of the partnership, if no contrary statement appears of record. A title company ordinarily will not insure title in a general partnership or its grantee until such statement has been recorded.

44.08 **NATURE OF PARTNER'S INTEREST**

A partner is co-owner with his partners of specific partnership property holding as a tenant in partnership. A partner's right in specific partnership property is not subject to dower, curtesy, or allowances to widows, heirs, or next of kin, **and is not community property.**

A partner's right in specific partnership property is not assignable, except in connection with the assignment of the rights of all the partners in the same property, and it is not subject to attachment, or execution, except on a claim against the partnership.

On the death of a partner his right in specific partnership property vests in the surviving partner or partners, except where the deceased was the last surviving partner, when it vests in his legal representative, such surviving partner or partners having no right to possess the partnership property for any but a partnership purpose.

A partner's interest in the partnership is his share of the profits and surplus, and the same is personal property.

A conveyance by a partner of his interest in the partnership entitles the assignee to receive, in accordance with his contract, the profits to which the assigning partner would otherwise be entitled, and in case of a dissolution of the partnership, the assignee is entitled to receive his assignor's interest.

A dissolution of the partnership is caused, among other ways, by: the death of any general partner; the bankruptcy of any general partner or the partnership; a decree of court under Section 15032, Corporations Code. The partnership is not terminated, however, until the partnership affairs have been wound up.

44.09 **SUMMARY, WITH REMINDERS TO ESCROW AND TITLE MEN WHEN HANDLING ORDERS INVOLVING PARTNERSHIPS**

A—**Prior to the adoption of the Uniform General and Limited Partnership Laws** on August 14, 1929, a partnership as such could not take the legal title to property, although the partners could as individuals. This was because a partnership, under the common law, was not considered a legal entity.

For example:

(a) A deed in favor of "Los Angeles Realty Company, a co-partnership" did not convey the legal title.

137

(b) A deed in favor of "Los Angeles Realty Company, a co-partnership, composed of John Jackson and James Jones," conveyed the legal title to said individuals. A deed out, to convey the full title, must be executed by all such individuals and their wives, and need not necessarily mention the partnership.

(c) A deed in favor of "John Jackson and Company" was held to convey the legal title to John Jackson.

B—Subsequent to the adoption of the Uniform Partnership Act of August 14, 1929, a partnership may acquire and convey real property in its own name.

(a) In a deed being drawn **to** a partnership so formed, the grantee's name should appear as, for example, "Merton Bros., a partnership." It is good practice to add: "composed of John Merton and William Merton, partners."

(b) In a deed being drawn **from** a partnership, the names of the partners need not be shown in the granting clause. The grantor's name should appear as: "Merton Bros., a partnership." It is good practice, however, to add: "composed of John Merton and William Merton, partners."
This deed should be signed by:

MERTON BROS, a partnership,

By _____ Partner

By _____ Partner

This deed should be acknowledged by the partnership in the form set out in Section 2.26.

(c) The wives of the partners need not join with the partners in deeds or other instruments affecting property of a partnership formed under said Act of August 14, 1929.

(d) In the case of a deed or other instrument executed by less than all of the partners, a special or general resolution adopted by all the partners or other evidence should be called for showing authorization for the particular act.

(If authorized, any partner may act for the partnership.)

(e) If the partnership is a **limited partnership,** it is not necessary that the "limited" partners join with the "general" partners in the execution of deeds and other instruments affecting real property. (Limited partners, as such, are not bound by the obligations of the partnership.)

(f) Judgments against individual partners are not a lien upon property acquired in the name of the partnership. (Federal tax liens, however, will not be ignored by a title company.)

(g) An **individual** doing business under a **fictitious name** is not a partnership and cannot acquire or convey real property in the "fictitious name." The deed should run in favor of, or be executed by, the **individual.** Following the individual's name there may be added, if desired, "doing business under the fictitious name of _____"

POWERS OF ATTORNEY

45.01 **DEFINITION**

An instrument in writing whereby one person (the principal) authorizes another (the attorney-in-fact) to act for him. The powers granted are determined by the express terms of the instrument itself; they are not implied, except in so far as may be necessary to carry out the powers expressly granted.

45.02 **CONSTRUING THE LANGUAGE OF A POWER OF ATTORNEY**

(The exact wording of the power in so far as it authorizes the particular act affecting the property should be carefully examined even though it be a "general" power.)

—Power to sell is not a power to convey.

—Power to mortgage does not imply a power to execute a trust deed, but power "to mortgage or otherwise encumber" or "to mortgage and hypothecate" is considered by most title companies to cover the execution of a trust deed.

—Power to transfer is not a power to mortgage.

—Power to sell and convey is not authority to exchange.

—Power "to make and execute conveyances" authorizes a transfer of real estate, but a power "to attend to all business affairs appertaining to real or personal estate" is too indefinite for that purpose.

—Power to "negotiate" a lease does not authorize the execution of a lease by the attorney-in-fact. Neither does a mere power to sell, without further authorization, ordinarily authorize the execution of a contract of sale.

—General words in a power of attorney are limited and controlled by particular terms. Thus where the authority to perform specific acts is given, and general words are also employed, the latter are limited to the particular acts authorized.

45.03 AN ATTORNEY-IN-FACT IS PROHIBITED FROM:

Making a gift deed.

Making a deed, mortgage or release without receiving a valuable consideration. (The full consideration should be stated in the instrument.)

Conveying or mortgaging property on which a declaration of homestead has been filed.

Dealing with his principal's property for his own benefit.

Delegating his authority, unless expressly authorized.

Deeding his principal's property to himself or releasing a mortgage made by himself to his principal, or mortgaging his principal's property to himself.

Making a partition, unless expressly authorized.

45.04 WHO MAY EXECUTE OR ACT UNDER A POWER OF ATTORNEY

In general, any person natural or artificial, who is competent to contract, may execute or act under a power of attorney, unless he has interests adverse to those of the principal of which the latter had no knowledge.

A corporation may give a power of attorney and become bound by the act of its agent. If authorized by its articles (that is, if acting as agent for another comes within the general scope of its business, although not stated in so many words) it may act as an attorney-in-fact. A partnership also may give a power of attorney.

A minor may act under a power of attorney, except that infants of tender years, lunatics, imbeciles and persons judicially declared incompetent are incapable of giving or acting under a power of attorney—although generally the principal cannot complain of the lack of mental capacity of one whom he has chosen to represent him.

45.05 RECORDING POWER OF ATTORNEY

If dealing with real property it must be in writing and for record purposes must be acknowledged. In general the fact that a power of attorney is not acknowledged or recorded does not affect its validity as between the parties.

45.06 RECORDING CERTIFIED COPY

When a power of attorney is once recorded, a certified copy thereof may be recorded in other counties with like effect as though the original were recorded. A revocation should be recorded in every county in which there is the record of the original or a certified copy of the power of attorney.

45.07 MANNER OF EXECUTING INSTRUMENTS

An attorney-in-fact must subscribe the name of his principal and his own name as attorney-in-fact, as "A" by "B," his attorney-in-fact. It is not sufficient to sign "B," attorney-in-fact for "A," as this is the contract of the agent only, the words "attorney-in-fact for 'A'" being merely descriptive of the person. A contrary rule prevails as to executors, administrators and guardians.

(As to form of acknowledgment, see Sections 2.22 and 2.24 under "Acknowledgments.")

45.08 JOINT POWERS

A power of attorney may be joint, or it may be several, or it may be joint and several. A power to several attorneys-in-fact with full power of substitution does not authorize one alone to act. If, under such power, he substitutes another in his place, such substitution probably renders the original attorney's power nugatory and prevents him from acting further, and a revocation of the substitution would not reinstate him.

Joint agents must act jointly, and one cannot delegate his authority to the other, unless expressly authorized, but when appointed by law, or to transact public business, a majority may act.

In the absence of qualifying terms, or other circumstances restraining the authority of the attorney-in-fact, a power of attorney given by several principals in general terms authorizes the attorney-in-fact to deal with the interest of each, either jointly with the interests of the others, or separately, that is, whatever interest both or either of the principals have in the property affected. (179 Cal. 1.)

45.09 TERMINATION OF A POWER OF ATTORNEY

A power of attorney (unless coupled with an interest in the subject of the agency) is terminated as to every person having notice thereof by:

A—Its revocation by the principal. (The instrument of revocation must be acknowledged or proved, certified and recorded in the same office as the power of attorney.)

B—Death of the principal.

C—Incapacity of the principal to contract.

However—since May 13, 1943, when Section 2356 of the Civil Code was amended—the authority of an attorney-in-fact is not terminated as to any person entering any bona fide transaction without actual knowledge of the death or incapacity of the principal

PUBLIC LANDS AND SPANISH
AND MEXICAN GRANTS

6.01 IMPORTANT DATES IN CALIFORNIA'S HISTORY

April 9, 1822—California, a Spanish possession since 1769, became a Mexican province, through act of the junta meeting that day. The Mexican empire, newly established, lasted only a few months and gave way to the Mexican national government.

February 2, 1848—Signing of the Treaty of Guadalupe Hidalgo, by which California became a part of the United States.

September 9, 1850—California was admitted to the Union.

6.02 SPANISH AND MEXICAN LAND GRANTS

Spanish occupation of California in 1769 vested the title to the land in the King of Spain. During the Spanish period concessions of ranch property were made, the first being before the end of the eighteenth century. These were in the nature of grazing permits, rather than absolute grants.

Between 1822 and 1846 the Mexican government granted many ranch titles, particularly after the year 1828, some of them being confirmatory of Spanish concessions. The greater number of ranchos were granted after secularization of the missions had been completed in 1836.

These grants, Spanish and Mexican, later were approved or disapproved by the Board of Land Commissioners appointed by Congress in 1851, or by the federal courts to which its decisions were appealed. Successful claimants received a confirmatory patent from the United States, which included all mineral rights.

6.03 PUEBLO LANDS IN LOS ANGELES

The pueblo of Los Angeles was founded by the Spaniards, under Felipe de Neve, September 4, 1781.

The City of Los Angeles was incorporated April 4, 1850. It succeeded to the pueblo rights. The title of the city to four square Spanish leagues—17,924 acres—was later confirmed.

The city passed an ordinance on April 15, 1854, providing for the conveyance of its title to all persons who had been in actual possession of pueblo lands for twelve years.

The present practice, if no deed from the city appears of record, is to bring a suit to quiet title against the city.

46.04 LANDS OWNED BY THE STATE OF CALIFORNIA

In addition to those lands in which the State of California has ownership, such as those under navigable streams or lakes or harbors or those between ordinary high tide and ordinary low tide, it owns certain lands granted it by the United States, principal among which are:

A—School Lands and Lieu Lands

By Act of March 3, 1853, Congress granted to the State of California, for school purposes, the 16th and 36th section in each township, not mineral in character and not otherwise disposed of. Title thereto vested in the state as soon as the survey by the surveyor-general was approved. (No patents from the United States to the state were issued.)

When these numbered sections had been disposed of prior to the Act or were otherwise unavailable, lands of equal area, known as "lieu lands," could be selected in their stead. "School" sections surrendered by the state to the United States could then be disposed of by the latter under the land laws.

Title to lands in sections 16 and 36 will not be insured by a title company without investigation being made to determine that they were not mineral in character. Only those not known to be mineral **at the time of the approval by the surveyor-general of the survey** could pass to the state.

In 1927 Congress granted the mineral school section not then in controversy to the states with the restriction (among others) that the state, in disposing of any of said sections, should reserve all coal and other minerals therein.

Patents issued by the state run to the original purchaser but inure to the benefit of the assignee.

B—**Swamp and Overflowed lands**—granted to the state September 28, 1850. Patents to the state were issued upon request of the governor and after approval of survey by the General Land Office.

C—Lands granted for university purposes and under the control of the **Regents of the University of California,** together with certain other lands granted to the state for other purposes.

46.05 SALE AND LEASING OF STATE LANDS

Under the **"State Lands Act of 1938,"** in effect June 11, 1938, jurisdiction over the administration, sale and leasing of remaining state lands was transferred to a newly created State Lands Commission. Under the Act, deposits of oil and minerals in state-owned land (except land acquired upon sale for delinquent taxes) were reserved to the state. Therefore, conveyances or patents of such land issued by the state could not transfer oils and minerals even if they contained no specific reservations. Under the Act the state could lease its lands for oil and gas development, but no oil derrick could be erected on tide lands. In 1941 the provisions of the Act were incorporated within the Public Resources Code.

46.06 UNITED STATES PUBLIC LANDS

United States public lands are divided into townships, six miles square, by lines running due north and south and others crossing them at right angles. The Humboldt Meridian governs in Northern California, Mount Diablo Meridian in Central California, and the San Bernardino Meridian in Southern California. Tiers of townships are arranged north and south of the established base lines.

In theory, each township contains 36 sections, numbered from 1 to 36 inclusive, commencing at the northeast corner of the township and proceeding west and east alternately, 6 sections to a tier; but in many cases Spanish or Mexican land grants cut into the townships, and, where this is the case, the sections or parts of sections which would fall in the ranchos are omitted from the government maps of the townships. Each full section (also in theory) is a mile square, or 80 chains on the four side lines, and contains 640 acres; but owing to the curvature of the earth's surface the townships are shorter on the north lines than on the south. Deficiencies or surplus resulting therefrom, or from surveyors' errors, are thrown into northern and western tiers of sections, fractional portions of sections being given lot numbers on the government plats. Many re-surveys of the public lands have been made which in some cases shift the township and section lines great distances from the position shown by the previous survey. In such situations it may be difficult to determine which survey controls in locating the position of lands described in a conveyance.

46.07 **FACTS ABOUT PATENTS**

A—Title by United States patent is title **by record. Delivery is unnecessary.**

B—A United States **homestead** ordinarily is the **separate property** of the patentee, being the gift of the Government.

C—One who has done everything necessary to entitle him to a patent may sell, convey, mortgage, lease, etc.

D—For copies of lost or unrecorded United States patents, or for information not obtainable at the local land office, write to the Director of the Bureau of Land Management, Dept. of Interior, at Washington, D. C.

46.08 **RAILROAD GRANTS**

To stimulate western railroad construction, grants of large areas of the public domain were made to railroads by acts of Congress. Patents were issued, some of which were later voided because of the prior existence of valid homestead or preemption rights or for other reasons, with protection, however, to bona fide purchasers from the railroad companies.

In addition to absolute grants of public lands, Congress gave railroad companies certain right of way lands, usually 200 feet in width, with additional lands for shops and station grounds. The title so acquired within the right of way was a limited fee, with a reversionary right remaining in the United States. After the Act of March 3, 1875, the grants of land to railroad companies for right of way purposes conveyed only an easement or right of way for railroad purposes, subject to defeasance and forfeiture if not used for such purposes. The authority of the railroad company to abandon or convey the right of way land so as to narrow the width of that right of way is restricted.

SCHOOL DISTRICTS

47.01 ANNEXATION OF TERRITORY

In general, upon annexation of territory to a city or incorporated town, comprising a different school district, the school property in the annexed territory passes under the management, control and operation of the board of education or board of school trustees of such city or town, and the title to such property automatically becomes vested, by operation of law, in the school district of such city or town.

For example: By the annexation of Hyde Park and of Eagle Rock to Los Angeles, the school districts of Hyde Park and of Eagle Rock passed out of existence, and the title to real property held by them became vested in the Los Angeles City School District of Los Angeles County. The proper vesting in a policy of title insurance for property deeded to one of these former districts, accordingly, is: "Los Angeles City School District of Los Angeles County." No reference need be made to the district by which title was acquired.

Section 2402 of The Education Code provides that "in the name by which the district is designated the trustees may sue and be sued, and hold and convey property for the use and benefit of the school district."

47.02 AUTHORITY OVER PROPERTY

School boards have power to manage and control school property within their districts, and, upon the

conditions prescribed by statute, to sell or lease real
property belonging to their respective districts. They
have power to dedicate property for public street pur
poses and to dedicate easements for water, sewer or
storm drain pipes.

(See The Education Code, enacted in 1943, and as
amended. Section 18600 et seq. covers the sale and leas
ing of real property.)

STATE GIFT TAX

48.01   Gifts of any property, or income therefrom, in trust
or otherwise, made after June 21, 1939, the effective
date of the "Gift Tax Act of 1939," are subject to a tax
imposed by the State of California. On July 1, 1945, it
became a part of the Revenue and Taxation Code. (See
Sections 15101, et seq.)

48.02   Donors are allowed certain specific exemptions
however, as under the State Interitance Tax Act. In addition, there is an annual exemption of gifts, not exceeding $4,000, to any one donee.

48.03   If the tax is not paid when due, the controller may
file for record in any county a certificate naming do
nor, donee and amount due. From the time of the recording of this certificate, the tax, with interest and
penalties, **is a lien upon any real property** in the county then owned or thereafter acquired by donor or
donee. This lien continues for ten years after delinquency or until paid. The controller has power to release and to subordinate.

48.04   The gift tax **is a lien on any personal property**
given, from the time of the gift until ten years **after the
tax becomes delinquent.** A sale by the donee, or his
successor in interest, to a bona fide purchaser for an
adequate consideration removes the lien from the property sold and causes it to attach to **all other personal
property of the donee,** including after acquired property, except any sold to a bona fide purchaser for an
adequate consideration.

48.05   A gift return must be made by the donor on or before the fifteenth day of April following the close of the calendar year in which the gift was made. The tax is due when the gift is made. It is delinquent when the determination of the controller fixing the amount of the tax becomes final.

48.06   The Act is administered by the state controller through the Inheritance Tax Department.

STATE PERSONAL INCOME TAX

49.01   **Lien.** The state personal income tax becomes a lien upon real property only from the date of recording an abstract of judgment or a copy of the judgment or a certificate, specifying the amount of the tax, penalty and interest, in the county in which the real property is situated, in accordance with the Revenue and Taxation Code.

The lien has the force, effect and priority of a judgment lien and continues for ten years from the date of recording.

The lien may be extended for successive periods of ten years by the recording of an abstract or copy of judgment or a new certificate within ten years of the previous recording. (Sections 18864 and 18883, Revenue and Taxation Code.)

49.02   This tax was created by "The Personal Income Tax Act of 1935," in effect June 13, 1935, and is administered now by the Franchise Tax Board, which has the right to release or subordinate the lien thereof. On July 1, 1945, it became part of the Revenue and Taxation Code.

STATE RETAIL SALES
AND USE TAX
(See Section 11.06F)

STATE UNEMPLOYMENT RELIEF TAX

51.01   The lien of this tax (due from employers under the Unemployment Insurance Act) when created by the recording of an abstract of judgment or a copy thereof continues for ten years from the date of entry. (Sections 1815, 1816, Unemployment Insurance Code.) The lien of such tax when created by the recording of a certificate continues for ten years from the date of filing, but the lien may be extended for successive periods of ten years by the recording of a new certificate within ten years of the preceding recording. (Section 1703, Unemployment Insurance Code.) The lien may be released or subordinated by the director under the provisions of Sections 1704, 1705 of said Code.

SUBDIVISIONS
(See "Maps and Subdivisions")

SUBORDINATION AGREEMENTS

52.01   Any instrument by which a mortgage, deed of trust, chattel mortgage or lien is subordinated or waived, as to priority, may be recorded, thereupon operating as constructive notice of its contents. (See Section 2934, C.C.) If a deed of trust is being subordinated, only the beneficiary or his assignee need execute the instrument.

52.02   If a deed of trust or mortgage is being subordinated, the fact of the subordination should be endorsed on the back of the note secured, in addition to the recording of a subordination agreement.

TAXES AND ASSESSMENTS
TAXES

(Also see Inheritance Tax; Federal Estate Tax; Gift Taxes; Federal Tax Liens; Corporation Franchise and other State Taxes.)

53.01 COUNTY AND CITY TAXES IN GENERAL

County taxes are assessed against all property subject thereto according to its value at noon on the first Monday in March of each year. Arrangements can be made by municipalities to have their taxes assessed and collected by the county officials, in which event the amounts are included in the bills for county taxes. In cases where municipal taxes are not included, the due dates, delinquency dates, sale dates, penalties and redemption periods vary in the different cities.

53.02 CALENDAR OF COUNTY TAXES

First Monday in March at noon: taxes become a lien.

First Day of November: the first installment, that is, all secured personal property taxes and one-half of realty taxes, becomes due. (Both installments, that is, all taxes, may be paid at that time.)

Tenth Day in December (at 5 P.M.): the first installment becomes delinquent. (At that time a 6 per cent penalty is added to the first installment.)

When December 10 falls on Saturday, Sunday or legal holiday, taxes become delinquent at 5 P.M. on the next business day.

First Day of February: the second installment becomes due.

Tenth Day in April (at 5 P.M.): the second installment becomes delinquent. (At that time a 6 per cent penalty on "all unpaid taxes," and $1.00 for advertising for each unpaid tax item except personal property, are added. (Effective July 1, 1962 the charge is $3.)

When April 10 falls on Saturday, Sunday or legal holiday, taxes become delinquent at 5 P.M. on the next business day.

June 8 (on or about): the delinquent tax list is published for three weeks, stating the date when the delinquent properties will be sold to the state for non-payment of taxes (about June 30), and the amount due.

Lands which are 5 years tax-delinquent are deeded to the state, subject thereafter to sale at public auction.

(The foregoing calendar does not include city taxes unless they are collected by the county tax collector.)

Of special interest to lenders, who pay taxes on real

estate from impounds collected from borrowers, are Sections 2615.5 and 2910.7 of the Revenue and Taxation Code, added September 7, 1955. These sections provide that:

"Any person who receives a tax bill respecting property which has been assessed to another and who has power, pursuant to written or oral authorization, to pay the taxes on behalf of another shall after the taxes have been paid in full and within 30 days of the receipt of the written request of the assessee, either deposit the original or a copy of the bill in the United States mail in an envelope addressed to the last known address of the assessee as shown on the bill, postage being prepaid, or deliver it otherwise to the assessee within said 30 days."

53.03 **SALE BY STATE**

On and after October 1, 1949, no sales at public auction of tax-sold property may be made until after it has been deeded to the state.

All properties which have been deeded to the state for delinquent taxes may be sold by the County Tax Collector under the provisions of Chapters 7 and 8, Part 6, Division 1, Revenue and Taxation Code, at any time when applied for and upon authorization of the State Controller.

A sale of the tax-deeded property may be made at public auction without any application from prospective purchasers.

Under Section 3771 et seq., Revenue and Taxation Code, a procedure is outlined by which any property which has been deeded for delinquent taxes or assessments to the state, which property has also been deeded for delinquent taxes or assessments to or for the account of any municipality, irrigation or reclamation district, or other public corporation or district, may be sold, **on the conditions prescribed,** to such municipality, district or public corporation.

53.04 **PROPERTY SUBJECT TO TAXATION AND EXEMPTIONS**

All the property within the state, not exempt under

the laws of the United States, is subject to taxation with certain exceptions, as: certain trees and vines; growing crops; property used exclusively for public schools; for free public libraries and free museums; certain orphan asylums, also church buildings, unless rented, and rent paid to owner; buildings and certain other property of educational institutions of collegiate grade, not conducted for profit; property belonging to the United States, the state, or any county or municipal corporation within the state; bonds, notes, shares of capital stock; all mortgages and debts secured by lien on real or personal property; cemetery lands and property, unless used or held for profit. There is also a personal property exemption to householders of $100.00, and a veteran's exemption of $1,000.00, to residents of this state. This exemption shall not apply to any veteran owning property of the value of $5,000 or more, or where the spouse of such veteran owns property of the value of $5,000 or more, or $10,000 community property. (This $1,000.00 exemption applies not only to the veteran, but to his widow, or, if there is no widow, then to the widowed mother, and to a pensioned widow, father and mother, resident of this state.)

There is also a "welfare exemption": Property used exclusively for religious, hospital, scientific or charitable purposes, owned and operated by community chests, funds, foundations or corporations organized and operated for religious, hospital, scientific or charitable purposes, is exempt from taxation under certain circumstances. Affidavits for the welfare exemption, with financial statements, must be filed in duplicate on or before April 1 of each year with the assessor.

Church officers, veterans, institutions of collegiate grade and orphan asylums, *i.e.*, all claimants except "welfare exemption" claimants, must make claim of exemption each year between noon on the first Monday in March and 5 P.M. on the first Monday in May.

As a prerequisite to the allowance of such exemptions, the interest of the claimant in the property must be of record on the lien date in the office of the recorder of the county in which the property is located.

Section 261 of the Revenue and Taxation Code was

amended in 1961 to permit a veteran who has an unre-corded interest in real property, consisting of a con-tract of sale, to qualify for the veterans' tax exemption by filing an affidavit with the assessor stating:

(a) That he purchased the real property pursuant to to such unrecorded contract of sale; and

(b) That under such unrecorded contract of sale, he is obligated and responsible for the payment of the taxes.

53.05 PRIORITY OF TAX LIENS

The lien of county taxes on real property is superior to contract liens. Thus a tax title, if valid, is superior to a mortgage.

So the lien of such taxes for a subsequent year is su-perior to that of taxes for a prior year.

53.06 SEGREGATION OF CURRENT TAXES

Application for segregation of current taxes is to be made to the **tax collector,** by amendment to Section 2803 of the Revenue and Taxation Code, effective Sep-tember 22, 1951. The section, as amended, now reads:

"Any person showing evidence by presentation of a duly executed and recorded deed, purchase contract, deed of trust, mortgage, or final decree of court of an interest in any parcel of real property, except posses-sory interests, which does not have a separate valuation on the roll, and who is not the owner or contract pur-chaser of the entire parcel as assessed, may apply to the tax collector to have the parcel separately valued on the roll for the purpose of paying current taxes."

Such application shall be made after the first Mon-day in July and before any payment but not after No-vember 30th—pursuant to Section 2804 of the Revenue and Taxation Code, as amended in 1957.

53.07 REDEMPTION

A—**Regular method.** (Section 4101 et seq., Revenue and Taxation Code)

Unpaid amount of tax plus tax collector's penalty

and costs shall be added to the amount necessary to redeem each parcel tax-sold for the year of sale, and to
each delinquent year thereafter on property sold to the
state subsequent to September 18, 1959, and:

(a) Redemption penalties of 1% per month from
July 1 of the year of sale for one year and ½ of
1% per month thereafter.

(b) On each subsequent delinquent year 1% per
month from July 1 for one year and ½ of 1% per
month thereafter.

(c) State redemption fee of $1.50 shall be added to
the amount necessary to redeem each parcel tax-
sold subsequent to June 13, 1947.

B—Permanent Five Year Installment Plan. (Sections
4216 to 4226, Revenue and Taxation Code.)

First installment: 20% or more of amount necessary
to redeem at the time election is made to pay under
this section.

Taxes for the fiscal year in which first payment is
made must be paid on or before April 10, except that
if election to pay in installments is made after April 10,
current taxes must be paid with or prior to installment
payment.

Subsequent installments: 20% or more of redemption amount and interest on balance of redemption
amount at ½ of 1% on the first day of each month,
from date of last payment.

Failure to pay an installment or current taxes on or
before April 10 of any fiscal year constitutes a default.

In case of default, election may not be made to again
pay until July 1 of the second succeeding fiscal year
after that in which such default occurs.

During the time payments are made under this plan,
there will be no sale by the state.

C—Credits in Case of Default or Substitution

Installments (including interest) paid under **de-
faulted** installment plan will be credited if:

(a) Redemption is made within five years of default. (Section 4336, Revenue and Taxation Code.)

(b) Election is made to pay under **new installment** plan. Such credit is not to be a substitute for
any installment, and shall be allowed after the first

installment is paid. (Section 4337, Revenue and Taxation Code)

53.08 PARTIAL REDEMPTION

Any person claiming an interest, evidenced by presentation of a duly executed and recorded deed, purchase contract, deed of trust, mortgage, or final decree of court, in any parcel of tax-sold or tax-deeded property which does not have a separate valuation on the roll for the year for which it became tax delinquent or any subsequent roll, and who is not the owner or contract purchaser of the entire parcel as assessed, may apply to the redemption officer to have the parcel separately valued in order that it may be redeemed. (Section 4151 Revenue and Taxation Code.)

53.09 PROPERTY THAT ESCAPES TAXATION

If any property belonging on the local roll has escaped assessment, the assessor shall assess the property on discovery at its value on the lien date for the year for which it escaped assessment if:

(a) The property is owned or controlled by the same person who owned or controlled it for the year for which it escaped assessment, or

(b) The only transfers made of the property since the lien date for the year for which the property escaped assessment have been transfers by gift, descent bequest, or devise. (Section 531, Revenue and Taxation Code.)

53.10 THE TAX YEAR AND THE PRO-RATING OF TAXES

Taxes become a lien at noon on the first Monday in March of each year, when the tax year begins, and are referred to as taxes of the current year, but the fiscal year is from July 1 following to June 30 of the next year, when the funds collected may be expended.

Pro-rating is a matter of agreement between the buyer and seller. Several plans have been adopted, based on the fiscal year.

The tax status at the time an escrow is closed determines the adjustment. For example: if the escrow i closed after July 1 and before the first half of taxes has been paid, the purchaser should receive as adjustment a pro-ration from July 1 to date of close of escrow, or to such other adjustment date as may be agreed upon. If, however, the first half of taxes has been paid by the seller, the seller should receive a pro-ration from the adjustment date to December 31 following, which latter date represents the end of the period covered by payment of the first half of taxes. If both installments have been paid, the seller should receive a rebate from the date of the adjustment date to the following June 30. All such adjustments are, of course, subject to any change upon which the parties may agree.

In adjusting a personal property tax, it must be borne in mind that while this tax is paid with the first half of the real property taxes it covers the payment for the full tax year.

In the event that the amount of taxes for the fiscal year is not available at the time the adjustment is to be made, the pro-ration is ordinarily based on the prior year's assessment.

53.11 **PERSONAL PROPERTY TAXES**

Secured personal property taxes become due and payable on November 1, with the first half of realty taxes. By resolution of the Board of Supervisors, a county may collect half of the personal property tax with each installment of the real property tax (since 1961).

Unsecured personal property taxes become due and payable to the county tax collector on the first Monday in March of each year and if unpaid are delinquent August 31st at 5 P.M., when a penalty of 8% is added. If August 31st falls on Saturday, the time of delinquency is 5 P.M. on the next business day.

(A tax on personal property is a lien on any real property on the secured roll also belonging to the owner of the personal property if the personal property is located upon such real property on the lien date, and if the fact of the lien is shown on the secured roll opposite the description of the real property. (Section 2189, Revenue and Taxation Code.)

53.12 TAX SALES TO INDIVIDUALS

Tax sales to individuals for state and county taxes (but not for city taxes) will be ignored by a title company if no tax deed has been issued. The last year of sales to individuals was 1893-94 under the former practice. Statutes 1907, Chap. 512, Political Code, Section 3785, required application for deed to be made prior to May 22, 1908. The deed, though issued, may not appear of record.

53.13 THIRTY-YEAR LIMIT ON TAX LIENS

The lien of every state or county tax ceases to exist after thirty years from the time the tax became a lien. Such tax shall be conclusively presumed then to have been paid unless the property subject thereto has been deeded for non-payment thereof. (Section 2195, Revenue and Taxation Code.)

53.14 TAX TITLES

Most title insurance companies, including Title Insurance and Trust Company, insure tax titles that meet their requirements. If one year has elapsed since the date of the state's deed to the purchaser, the deed can ordinarily be insured, provided the former owner is not in possession, current taxes have been paid, and no serious defects are shown in the company's examination of all the proceedings leading up to the state's deed.

On and after October 1, 1949, the holder of a tax title must be reimbursed for permanent improvements made—as well as for tax redemption costs involved—if the tax deed is held void. (Sections 3728, Revenue and Taxation Code, as amended.)

53.15 TAX SALE MORATORIUM

The moratorium on tax sales that had been extended by the 1947 legislature was ended October 1, 1949, by the repeal of Sections 3490 to 3494, inclusive, of the

Revenue and Taxation Code, which provided for the same.

ASSESSMENTS

53.16 The general tax bill includes various special district assessments, such as fire protection, garbage disposal, library, lighting, county water, etc. In some municipalities it may also include certain street improvement assessments.

There are many street improvement and other assessments, however, that are not included in the general tax bill. As to such, **those in an amount less than $25.00** are payable in cash. Under the Improvement Act of 1911, for example, if such assessments are unpaid after thirty days from the date of the recording of the assessment they draw interest and ultimately penalties and a suit to foreclose the lien.

53.17 **As to those assessments that are $25.00 or more in amount,** bonds are issued if the assessments are unpaid thirty days from the date of recording. (Division 7, Part 5, Chapter 2 of the Streets and Highways Code, however, allows a lot owner who desires no bond to be issued to notify the treasurer of his desires, presenting to him, at the same time, an affidavit of ownership, and a certificate of a searcher of records.)

Bonds for city improvements are payable at the city treasurer's office and for county improvements at the county treasurer's office.

Under the provisions of Section 2911 of the Civil Code, effective September 15, 1945, the lien of an assessment or bond is presumed to be extinguished four years after the due date of the assessment or bond or four years after the last installment thereof or of the last principal coupon attached to the bond, or on January 1, 1947, whichever is later.

53.18 Many street improvements are carried out under the Improvement Act of 1911. The Opening and Widening Act, the Boundary Line Act and the Acquisition and Improvement Act of 1925 (Mattoon Act) have also been much used. Under the latter Act, which was repealed August 21, 1933, assessments were levied, not against particular parcels, but against the entire district divided into zones, and were collected with taxes. There are acts in effect, also, providing for the refunding and readjustment of the indebtedness of Mattoon Act districts.

53.19   **Irrigation District assessments** are levied against the property in the district and are to take care of the principal and interest on bonds issued by the district and to maintain and operate the property and works of the district. They are a lien on land and are payable to the district collector.

TIDE LANDS AND
SUBMERGED LANDS

54.01   See "Accretion," 1.01 et seq., and see "Lands Owned By State of California," 46.04.

TORRENS TITLES

55.01   **THE TORRENS SYSTEM**

The Land Title Act, commonly called the Torrens Act, in effect from December 19, 1914 to April 30, 1955, provided a system of land registration in California. By an emergency measure effective April 30, 1955, at 9 A.M., the Land Title Act was repealed. With repeal Torrens registration in California ended.

Torrens registers, files, documents, indices, books, and records then became a part of the records of the offices of California's county recorders—though without "any greater or other effect as constructive notice or otherwise" than at time of registration.

Thereafter documents affecting formerly registered land must be recorded in the usual manner meeting only the usual recorder's requirements and subject only to the usual recorder's fees.

Since November 7, 1950, and prior to the repeal of the Act, it was possible for an owner of registered land to withdraw from the Torrens system if he wished to do so.

TRUSTS
(Also see "Trust Deeds.")

56.01 DEFINITION

While the word "trust" is variously used and applied to different relationships, its general meaning is to designate the arrangement or transaction by which property is transferred to one person to be held and administered by him for the benefit of another.

56.02 PARTIES

The person who creates a trust is called the trustor; the person who holds title and administers the trust is called the trustee; and the person for whose benefit the trust is created is called the beneficiary.

56.03 TRUSTS CLASSIFIED

A trust is either: voluntary (that is, one voluntarily accepted by the trustee); or involuntary (that is, one created by operation of law).

56.04 CREATION

No trust **in relation to real property** is valid unless created or declared:

A—By a written instrument, subscribed by the trustee, or by his agent thereto authorized by writing;

B—By the instrument under which the trustee claims the estate affected;

C—By operation of law.

56.05 PURPOSES OF EXPRESS TRUSTS

A—Prior to August 14, 1929, express trusts in **relation to real property** could be only those specified in Section 857 of the Civil Code.

B—On and after August 14, 1929, a trust in relation to real and personal property, or either of them, may be created for any purpose or purposes for which a contract may be made.

56.06 EFFECT OF DECLARATION OF TRUST

The nature, extent and object of a trust are expressed in the declaration of trust (that is, the instrument by which it is created).

56.07 SUFFICIENCY OF INSTRUMENT TO CREATE TRUST

No technical language is necessary to create a trust, either by will or deed, and any expression that shows unequivocally the intention to do so will have that effect, although the words "trust" or "trustee" are not used, provided it is otherwise sufficient and the trust is valid.

The language must be reasonably definite and certain as to the intention to create a trust, and as to the subject, purpose and beneficiary of the trust. (Civil Code, Sections 2221-22. 124 Cal. 418.)

56.08 EFFECT OF VOID TRUST

Where there is a clear intention to create a trust, but the trust is void for any reason, either no title passes, or a resulting trust remains in favor of the grantor, since a trustee takes only such estate as is necessary to carry out the trust. But if a consideration passed, then the trustee holds under a resulting trust for the person who paid the consideration.

56.09 POWERS OF TRUSTEE

A trustee has only such powers as are expressly given him, and such as are necessarily implied to enable him to carry out the objects and purposes of the trust. A court in equity, however, may raise new powers. (**Adams v. Cook,** 15 Cal. (2d) 352.)

A trustee under a testamentary trust may petition the Probate Court for authority to exercise powers not previously conferred upon him. (Section 1120, Probate Code) If the petition is filed on or after September 9, 1953, and the statutory procedure followed, an order granting new powers to the testamentary trustee may be relied upon. Section 1120 was amended in 1959 to provide that the Probate Court may authorize a testamentary trustee to accept additions to the trust from sources other than the decedent's estate.

A trustee may lease the trust property, under certain conditions, beyond the term of the trust, as provided by Section 2272, Civil Code, added September 19, 1947. If the trust is testamentary, an order authorizing or confirming the lease must be procured under Section 1120, Probate Code.

56.10 SUCCESSION OR APPOINTMENT OF NEW TRUSTEE

The superior court shall appoint a trustee whenever there is a vacancy and the declaration of trust does not provide a practical method of appointment. (Sections 2287, 2289 C.C.)

On the death, renunciation, or discharge of one of several co-trustees the trust survives to the others. (Sections 2288, 860, C.C.)

56.11 DEALING WITH HIMSELF

A trustee cannot, in his official capacity, deal with himself in his individual capacity.

He cannot release or assign a mortgage made by himself in favor of the trust estate without first obtaining an order of court authorizing the same. Neither can he convey or mortgage trust property to himself or to his wife.

56.12 DURATION

A trust—except a strictly charitable one—cannot endure for a longer period "than 21 years after some life in being at the creation of the interest and any period of gestation involved in the situation to which the limitation applies. The lives selected to govern the time of vesting must not be so numerous or so situated that evidence of their deaths is likely to be unreasonably difficult to obtain. It is intended by the enactment of this section to make effective in this State the American common law rule against perpetuities."

(Section 715.2, added to the Civil Code Sept. 22, 1951.)
A strictly charitable trust may endure perpetually.

56.13 **ACTIONS**

As legal title is vested in the trustee for the purposes of the trust, the trustee is ordinarily a proper party to any action affecting the trust property.

When sued as an individual merely, personal interests only, and not the trust estate or powers, are affected thereby.

Where an action affects only the beneficial interests under the trust, the title and estate of the trustee are not affected thereby.

In actions against the trust property, in addition to the trustee, the beneficiaries should be parties defendant unless it is expressly provided in the declaration that the trustee shall represent the beneficiaries in litigation involving the trust or the trust property.

TRUSTS—COMMON LAW SYNDICATES

57.01 **OWNERSHIP OF REAL PROPERTY**

Common law "syndicates," "companies," or "trusts," for the transaction of business of various kinds, operating under the provisions of so-called trust agreements, frequently termed "Massachusetts Trusts," sometimes "Hulbert Plan Trusts," are usually organized as substitutes for corporations.

The title to any property they hold is vested in trustees, the legality of the acts of the trustees being dependent upon the legality of the trust agreement or declaration from which they draw their powers and the provisions thereof.

If the trustees do not take control of the trust property under, and draw their powers from, the trust instrument alone, but are under the control of the beneficiaries or share-holders, then probably a partnership, and not a trust, is created.

It has been held that a sale by the trustees, without a permit from the corporation commissioner, of units, shares or interests in such a common law trust is a violation of the Corporate Securities Act, or so-called Blue Sky Law. (186 Cal. 718.)

57.02 ATTITUDE OF TITLE COMPANIES

A title vested in a common law trust may be insured if the trust is valid, as disclosed by an examination of the recorded trust agreement or declaration of trust, provided the deed runs in favor of the trustees as trustees for the trust, and provided a statement describing the trust has been filed with the Franchise Tax Board at Sacramento. (Said trusts, like corporations, are subject to the corporation franchise tax and corporation income tax.) The acts of the trustees under a trust that meets the foregoing requirements may also be insured.

TRUST DEEDS

(Also see Bond Issues by Corporations; Corporate Securities Act; Moratorium; Mortgages; Deficiency Judgments; Trusts.)

58.01 DEFINITION

A trust deed is a conveyance of property to a person or corporation as trustee, for the purpose of securing a debt or other obligation, with a power of sale in the trustee, upon default, to apply the proceeds in payment thereof.

58.02 DISTINGUISHED FROM MORTGAGES

A mortgage is merely a lien upon the land, the mortgagor retaining the entire legal title. It must be foreclosed by action, unless it contains a power of sale —in which event it may also be foreclosed by action. The statute of limitations applies and on foreclosure the statutory right of redemption exists.

On the other hand **a trust deed conveys the legal title** to the trustee and it remains in him until the debt is paid, or a sale is made upon default. (149 Cal. 320.) He may, therefore, foreclose under the power of sale conferred upon him. The statute of limitations does not affect his powers and there is no statutory or other right of redemption after sale, unless the foreclosure is by court action.

Whether an instrument is a trust deed or a mortgage is to be determined by the nature of the transaction with respect to **whether a trust is created or not.**

In case of doubt the instrument will be considered a mortgage. (135 Cal. 277.)

The so-called "trust deed or mortgage" to secure a bond issue, providing for foreclosure by sale by the trustee or by a court action, is ordinarily treated as a mortgage with power of sale and foreclosed by action, in which case the statutory right of redemption exists, or by exercise of the power of sale without right of redemption. Sometimes such instruments are termed "mortgages in trust." (17 Cal. Jur. 723.) If foreclosed by action, the question whether they are technically trust deeds or mortgages is immaterial. (60 Cal. App. 568.)

58.03 IMPORTANT FACTS IN GENERAL

A—A trust deed may by its terms cover **after acquired property** of the trustor. (But if said trust deed is recorded before the trustor acquires title, its recordation will not constitute constructive notice to innocent purchasers dealing with the trustor, after acquisition of title, in good faith, for value, and without actual notice of such trust deed.)

B—A trust deed **note may be dated** prior or subsequent to the trust deed.

C—The **legal rate of interest** is 7 per cent, but the parties may, by express provision, agree to pay not to exceed 10 per cent per annum (with certain exceptions, as to which see topic of Usury).

D—A trust deed **note may be assigned** either absolutely or as collateral security by an endorsement on the back of the note. On and after August 14, 1931, however, any assignment of the beneficial interest under a deed of trust may be recorded and from the time the same is filed for record operates as constructive notice of the contents thereof.

E—**Formal acceptance** of the trust by the trustee is unnecessary where he in fact accepts and acts under its provisions.

F—For **advances**, see Section No. 41.02, Paragraph C.

G—**Effect of failure of wife to join** in execution of trust deed. See under topic of Mortgages, Section No. 41.07, as the same rules apply.

H—**In any action affecting a trust deed** both the trustee and beneficiary of record should be made parties.

I—For trust deeds by **religious, social or benevolent corporations,** see Sections Nos. 11.12, 11.13, 59.01, 59.02.

J—For trust deeds given to secure a **bonded indebtedness,** see topic of BOND ISSUES BY CORPORATIONS, Section No. 7.01 et seq.

K—Trust deeds covering a minor's or incompetent's interest can be executed only upon proper order of court.

L—Personal property (including trust deeds) acquired by a married woman on or after July 29, 1927 (other than by gift, bequest, devise, descent, or by assignment from her husband—which is her separate property) is **presumptively separate property.**

M—For extensions of trust deed notes see under topic of **Extensions** under **Mortgages.** (Section No. 41.05.)

N—For **assignments or partial reconveyances** executed by administrators or executors, see Section 41.02-B.

O—A trust deed may run in favor of "owner and holder of the note hereby secured" and the note may run in favor of "bearer."

P—**Fictitious mortgages** and **deeds of trust** of real property may be recorded with the county recorder, as provided in Section 2952, Civil Code, in effect September 19, 1947. They need not be acknowledged, but they must bear a notation on the face that they are fictitious. After recording, any of the provisions may be included **by reference** in any mortgage or deed of trust recorded in the same county. The reference must comply with the requirements of said Section 2952.

58.04 LEGAL EFFECT OF TRUST DEED

While a trust deed does not merely create a lien or encumbrance on the land, but conveys to the trustee the entire legal title for the purpose of the trust, yet, under the rule that a trustee takes only such estate as is necessary to the execution of the trust, the title of the trustee lies dormant until the necessity for foreclosure arises, and prior to that time has none of the legal incidents of ownership. Hence, he need not give notice of non-responsibility under the Mechanics' Lien Law. (155 Cal. 270.) Prior to foreclosure, the trustor, or his successors, can convey, mortgage, homestead, or otherwise deal with the property, subject, however, to the trust deed. (153 Cal. 771.)

58.05 RIGHT TO SUE ON THE INDEBTEDNESS

Where the remedy by trustee's sale has been exhausted, the creditor may sue on the note for any deficiency (with certain exceptions), unless the statute of limitations has run, and subject to restrictions imposed by law. (See topic of Deficiency Judgments, Section No. 31.10.)

58.06 CREDITOR OR BENEFICIARY AS TRUSTEE

The creditor may act as trustee. (7 Cal. App. 379.) He may also purchase at his own sale, **if the trust deed so provides;** but otherwise the debtor may redeem—this being an exception to the general rule that purchase by a trustee at his own sale is void. (133 Cal. 659.)

58.07 APPOINTMENT OF TRUSTEE BY COURT

Sections 2287 and 2289 of the Civil Code, providing that the Superior Court must appoint a trustee whenever there is a vacancy, and the declaration of trust does not provide a practical method of appointment, applies to trustees under deeds of trust. (158 Cal. 390.)

Section 2287 also provides that, other things being equal, the court shall give preference to the nominee of beneficiaries of the trust who are over fourteen years of age.

58.08 **SUBSTITUTION OF TRUSTEES IN TRUST DEEDS**

A—Section 2934a of the Civil Code, enacted on September 15, 1935, provides that the trustee under a trust deed may be substituted by the recording in the county in which the property is located of a substitution executed and acknowledged by all of the beneficiaries under said trust deed, or their successors in interest.

A copy of the substitution must be mailed, prior to the recording thereof, in the manner provided in Section 2924b of the Civil Code, to all persons to whom a copy of the notice of default would be required to be mailed by the provisions of said Section 2924b. The substitution must contain date and book and page of trust deed, names of trustee, trustor and beneficiary and name of new trustee. It must have attached an affidavit that notice has been given as required above. It must also contain an acknowledgment by the trustee named in the trust deed of a receipt of a copy thereof or an affidavit of personal service of a copy thereof, or of publication of notice in accordance with Section 6061 of the Government Code. Where service is by publication, the affidavit shall also show that a copy of such substitution has been mailed to said trustee at his last known address.

The provisions of Section 2934a of the Civil Code do not appear to be applicable to any trust deed containing a power of substitution or prescribing the manner in which substitution shall be made, irrespective of the date of execution of such trust deed. Only those trust deeds not containing such a power of substitution and executed subsequent to September 15, 1935, would be subject to the provisions of said code section.

B—The trustor and beneficiary (or their successors in interest) may, by a proper instrument, substitute a trustee. (37 Cal. App. (2) 307.)

58.09 EFFECT OF CONVEYANCE FROM TRUSTOR TO TRUSTEE

A deed from the trustor to the trustee does not necessarily merge the title.

58.10 RECONVEYANCE WHEN TRUST DEED OR NOTE IS LOST

If the trust deed or note secured thereby is lost, a responsible trustee will not execute a reconveyance, when called upon do so, unless a surety bond is furnished and then only after an exhaustive search has been made for the missing document.

58.11 FORECLOSURE PRIOR TO JULY 28, 1917

Prior to July 28, 1917, there was no statutory regulation of trustee's sales. All procedure relating thereto was wholly a matter of contract between the parties, as expressed in the trust deed. It was only necessary to follow explicitly the provisions thereof. The sale had to be made in accordance with the provisions of the trust deed. (175 Cal. 272.)

58.12 FORECLOSURE AFTER JULY 27, 1917

As to trust deeds or mortgages with power of sale executed **after July 27, 1917, the power of sale cannot be exercised** except under Section 2924 of the Civil Code which, as amended, provides:

Where, by a mortgage created after July 27, 1917, of any estate in real property, other than an estate at will or for years, less than two, or in any transfer in trust made after July 27, 1917, of a like estate to secure the performance of an obligation, a power of sale is conferred upon the mortgagee, trustee, or any other person, to be exercised after a breach of the obligation for which such mortgage or transfer is a security, **such power shall not be exercised** (except where such mortgage or transfer is made pursuant to an order, judgment, or decree of a court of record, or to secure the payment of bonds or other evidences or indebtedness authorized or permitted to be issued by the commissioner of corporations, or is made by a public utility subject to the provisions of the Public Utilities Act) **until the following procedure has been complied with:**

58.13 A—A Notice of Default must be filed

The trustee, mortgagee, or beneficiary, shall first **file for record,** in the office of the recorder of **each county** wherein the mortgaged or trust property or some part or parcel thereof is situated, a notice of default, identifying the mortgage or deed of trust by stating the name or names of the trustor or trustors and giving the book and page where the same is recorded or a description of the mortgaged or trust property and containing a statement that a breach of the obligation for which such mortgage or transfer in trust is security has occurred, and setting forth the nature of such breach and of his election to sell or cause to be sold such property to satisfy the obligation.

(Prior to August 21, 1933, the notice of default did not have to set forth the nature of the default or the name or names of the trustor or trustors.)

Mailing of the notice of default upon a **recorded request made on or after August 21, 1933,** is required, also, in addition to recordation. See Section 58.17 following for details.

Publication of the notice of default or **personal delivery** of a copy to trustor or mortgagor must be made, also, in addition to recordation, in the case of certain deeds of trust and mortgages with power of sale **executed after September 19, 1939.** See Section 58.17.

B—Three Months after the Filing of the Notice of Default Must Elapse

C—A Notice of Sale Must be Given

After such elapse of three months, the mortgagee, trustee or other person authorized to make the sale shall give notice of sale, stating the time and place thereof, in the manner and for a time not less than that required by law for sales of real property upon execution. (Prior to September 19, 1939, there was no specific requirement that three months must first elapse before giving such notice. Sales held on or after September 19, 1939, will not be insured by a title company unless the full three months elapsed before the beginning of publication and posting of notice of the sale.) See Section 58.15-C following.

58.14 FORECLOSURE BY COURT ACTION

The beneficiary or trustee in a deed of trust or mortgagee in a mortgage with power of sale upon real property or any interest therein (or the successor or successors in interest of such beneficiary, trustee or mortgagee) has the **right to bring suit to foreclose the same in the manner and subject to the provisions, rights and remedies relating to the foreclosure of a mortgage.** (725a, C.C.P., in effect August 21, 1933, and as amended September 13, 1941.)

If this right is exercised the real property sold under a decree of foreclosure may be **redeemed** within **three months after the sale**—unless the sale be for less than the judgment sum, in which latter event the redemption period is **one year.** (725a, C.C.P., as amended September 19, 1939.) Prior to the amendment of 1939 the redemption period was twelve months. This amendment of 1939 would appear to apply only to deeds of trust executed on or after September 19, 1939, in so far as the three-months' redemption period is concerned.

Prior to August 21, 1933, it was doubtful whether the ordinary deed of trust could be foreclosed by court action except where the accounts were unsettled or where the trustee refused to act or where there were other special reasons.

58.15 MANNER OF POSTING AND PUBLISHING NOTICE OF SALE

A—If the trust deed was executed prior to July 27, 1917, a notice of sale must be posted and published in such manner, and for such length of time, as the trust deed specifies. Such trust deeds usually provide merely for publication of the notice once (or twice) each week for a certain number of weeks in some newspaper of general circulation published in Los Angeles County (or in the county where the property is situated), or in both counties. Sometimes they also provide for mailing a copy of the notice to the trustor, and if so, this must also be done in the manner required.

B—If the trust deed was executed **on or after July 27, 1917,** in addition to complying with all provisions of the trust deed, notice of the time and place of sale must be given "in the manner and for a time not less than that required by law for sales of real property under execution." (Such trust deeds usually contain merely this general provision in the language of said section.)

C—Section 692 C.C.P., provides that notice of sale of real property on execution or power contained in any deed of trust or mortgage must be given as follows:

(a) By **posting written notice** of the time and place of sale, properly describing the property, for **twenty days** (before date of sale) in one public place in the city where the property is to be sold, if the property is to be sold in a city, or, if not, then in one public place in the **judicial district** ("township" prior to January 1, 1952) in which the property is to be sold.

Prior to August 14, 1931, and on and after August 17, 1923, the code required the posting of the notice in **three** public places of the township or city where the property was to be sold. Prior to August 17, 1923, the notice had to be posted also in **three** public places of the township or city where the property was **situated.**

(b) Also, by **publishing** a copy of said notice once a week for the same twenty-day period in some newspaper of general circulation printed and published in the city in which the property or some part thereof is situated, if any part thereof is situated in a city, if not, then in some newspaper of general circulation printed and published in the **judicial district** ("township" prior to January 1, 1952) in which the property or some part thereof is situated, or, in case no newspaper of general circulation be printed and published in the city or judicial district ("township" prior to January 1, 1952), as the case may be, in some newspaper of general circulation printed and published in the county. (If property is in two cities, publication in one is sufficient.)

(c) Also, if the property is to be sold under the provisions of any deed of trust, or under power of sale contained in a mortgage or where real property is to be sold under execution upon a judgment, by **posting a copy of said notice** in some conspicuous place **on the property to be sold,** at least twenty days before the sale. (This provision does not apply to sales made prior to August 17, 1923.)

58.16 PLACE OF SALE

A sale under execution or deed of trust executed after August 14, 1931, must be held in the county where the property or some part thereof is situated.

58.17 SPECIAL REQUIREMENTS AS TO THE GIVING OF NOTICE OF DEFAULT AND NOTICE OF SALE UNDER SECTION 2924b, C.C.

A copy of the notice of default and a copy of the notice of sale must be mailed to anyone requesting it **on or after August 21, 1933,** if a duly acknowledged **request** is filed for record in the office of the recorder of any county in which any part or parcel of the real property is situated. This request must identify the deed of trust (in accordance with Section 2924b Civil Code) and must be filed subsequent to the recordation of deed of trust and prior to the recordation of the notice of default. A reference to the record of this request must be entered by the recorder upon the margin of the record of the deed of trust.

Within 10 days following recordation of the notice of default, a copy of the notice of default must be sent by registered mail by the trustee or beneficiary to the person or persons requesting it.

Furthermore, at least 20 days before the date of sale

the trustee or beneficiary must send a copy of the notice of the time and place of the sale, by registered mail, to the same person or persons.

Requests for notice may be contained in deeds of trust executed on or after August 21, 1933. These are as effective as if they had been filed separately.

If **no address** of the trustor or mortgagor is set forth in a deed of trust or mortgage with power of sale **executed after September 19, 1939,** and no request recorded by him, a copy of the notice of default shall be published once a week for at least four weeks in a newspaper of general circulation in the county in which the property is situated, such publication to commence within ten days after the filing of the notice of default. In lieu of such publication a copy of the notice of default may be **delivered personally** to the trustor or mortgagor within such ten days or at any time before publication is completed.

A recital in the deed, executed pursuant to the power of sale, that compliance has been made with all requirements regarding mailing of copies of notices for which requests have been recorded or the publication of a copy of the notice of default or of personal delivery of the copy of the notice of default shall constitute prima facie evidence of compliance therewith and conclusive evidence thereof in favor of bona fide purchasers and encumbrances for value and without notice. (Section 2924, Civil Code)

58.18 **REINSTATEMENT**

At any time within 3 months of the recording of the notice of default—or at any time prior to entry of the decree of foreclosure—the trustor or mortgagor or his successor in interest, or any beneficiary under a subordinate deed of trust or any other person having a subordinate lien or encumbrance of record, may reinstate the deed of trust or mortgage by the payment of the entire amount then due (other than such portion of principal as would not then be due had no default occurred), including costs and fees (trustee's or attorney's fees actually incurred not exceeding $100.00 in case of a mortgage, and $50.00 in case of a deed of trust or ½ of 1% of the entire unpaid principal sum secured, whichever is greater).

This applies only to deed of trust or mortgages executed on or after August 21, 1933—except that, as to the holders of subordinate liens, they may only reinstate a deed of trust or mortgage that is executed on or after September 22, 1951.

(Section 2924c, added to the Civil Code by Statutes 1933, as amended 1949, 1951, and 1957)

58.19 PENDENCY OF BANKRUPTCY PROCEEDINGS

During the pendency of bankruptcy proceedings by or against the trustor or the owner of the property, it has been held that the consent of the referee or bankruptcy court should be obtained to the foreclosure of the trust deed, or the sale may be void, or at least subject to the right of the trustee in bankruptcy to discharge the indebtedness and take the property. (214 Fed. 260; 104 Fed. 762; 206 Fed. 789; 236 Fed. 407.)

58.20 TRUSTEE'S DEED

After making the sale the trustee executes a deed to the purchaser. This deed should contain full recitals in regard to all matters connected with the sale, including a reference to the trust deed by book and page of record, a statement as to the default, recording notice of default and election to sell, with book and page of record, posting and publishing notices of sale, with dates, places and name of newspaper, time, place and manner of making sale, name of purchaser and full consideration received—in brief, everything that, under the provisions of the trust deed and of law, is necessary to make a valid sale.

If the trust deed provides that the recitals in the trustee's deed shall be conclusive, it has been held that they are conclusive in favor of third parties and even as between the trustor and beneficiary. (7 Cal. (2) 596.)

But see Sections 21.02 (Federal tax liens) and 36.14, 36.15 (mechanics' liens).

58.21 CORRECTION DEED

The trustee may execute a new deed to cure defective recitals in a former deed. (124 Cal. 169.)

58.22 AS TO EFFECT OF MECHANICS' LIENS

See under topic of Mechanics' Liens.

58.23 EFFECT OF VOID OR IRREGULAR SALES

It has been held that a power of sale given in a trust deed or mortgage is exhausted by one attempted exercise of it, so that, if the sale proves invalid, the power will not authorize a new sale.

But, according to the weight of authority, the power is not exhausted by a sale which is entirely void, or fails to pass the legal title. (41 Cor. Jur. 1035.)

Acquiescence for any considerable time in a sale which is voidable only, unless explained, is deemed a waiver, and ignorance of facts is not sufficient if due to the fault or negligence of the party seeking relief. But it is generally held that if the sale is fatally defective, it will be set aside and the trust deed reinstated.

Where the rights of third persons are not interfered with, the parties concerned may agree to disregard a sale that is invalid or irregular, and proceed to a new sale, and they will be estopped to question the validity of the new sale. (40 Cal. App. 424.)

58.24 WHEN A TRUSTOR COMES BACK INTO TITLE FOLLOWING A FORECLOSURE

(See Section 41.10.)

58.25 THE STATE AS A PARTY IN FORECLOSURE ACTIONS

(See Section 22.06.)

58.26 WAIVER BY BORROWER OF HIS RIGHTS

Section 2953 C.C. in effect August 27, 1937, and as amended September 19, 1939, and September 13, 1941, provides:

Any express agreement made or entered into by a borrower at the time of or in connection with the making of or renewing of any loan secured by a deed of trust, mortgage or other instrument creating a lien on real property, whereby the borrower agrees to waive the rights, or privileges conferred upon him by Sections 2924, 2924b, 2924c of the Civil

Code or by Sections 580a or 726 of the Code of Civil Procedure, shall be void and of no effect. The provisions of this section shall not apply to any deed of trust, mortgage or other liens given to secure the payment of bonds or other evidences of indebtedness authorized or permitted to be issued by the commissioner of corporations, or is made by a public utility subject to the provisions of the Public Utilities Act.

Said Section 2953 does not apply after the loan is made when all rights have been established, and there remains only the enforcement of those rights.

58.27 **DEFICIENCY JUDGMENTS**
(See Section 31.10.)

UNINCORPORATED BENEVOLENT OR FRATERNAL SOCIETIES OR ASSOCIATIONS AND UNINCORPORATED LABOR ORGANIZATIONS

59.01   Sections 21200 and 21201 of the Corporations Code provide:

"21200. Any unincorporated benevolent or fraternal society or association, and every lodge or branch of any such society or association, and any labor organization, may, without incorporation, purchase receive, own, hold, lease, mortgage, pledge, or encumber, by deed of trust or otherwise, manage, and sell all such real estate and other property as may be necessary for the business purposes and objects of the society, association, lodge, branch, or labor organization, subject to the laws and regulations of the society, association, lodge, or branch and of the grand lodge, thereof, or labor organization; and also may take and receive by will or deed all property

178

not so necessary, and hold it until disposed of with-in a period of ten years from the acquisition thereof.

"21201. All conveyances transferring or in any manner affecting the title to real estate owned or held by an unincorporated benevolent or fraternal society or association, or lodge or branch thereof, or labor organization, shall be executed by its presiding officer and recording secretary under its seal after resolution duly adopted by the society, association, lodge, or branch authorizing the conveyance."

Section 21202 of the Corporations Code defines "labor organization" as "any organization of any kind, or any agency or employee representation committee or plan, in which employees participate and which exists for the purpose in whole or in part, of dealing with employees concerning grievances, labor disputes, wages, rates of pay, hours of employment, or conditions of work."

59.02 When passing upon an instrument executed by an unincorporated society, association, lodge, or labor organization, a title company will call for its by-laws to see that the proper officers have executed it and to see what restrictions have been placed upon their acts. Resolutions must be called for showing that all require-ments have been met and that the particular deed, mortgage or other instrument is authorized. Particular care will be taken to determine that the organization is such an association as comes within the purview of the Code.

UNITED STATES INTERNAL REVENUE STAMPS

60.01 A deed, instrument or writing conveying real prop-erty requires revenue stamps if the consideration or value of the interest or property conveyed, exclusive of the value of any lien or encumbrance remaining thereon at the time of sale, exceeds $100.00. (26 U.S.C.A. Sec. 4361)

60.02   The **rate** is 55 cents if the consideration or value does not exceed $500.00 and 55 cents for each addition $500.00 or fractional part thereof.

60.03   An **encumbrance** existing at the time of the conveyance and not removed in the transaction **may be deducted** in computing the tax, but a purchase money mortgage or deed of trust cannot be deducted.

60.04   **Taxes and assessments** which are a lien and unpaid at the time of sale are deductible in computing the tax.

60.05   In the case of a **deed in lieu of foreclosure** the tax is calculated upon the amount of the debt, plus accrued interest and any additional consideration.

60.06   A **deed made pursuant to a contract of sale** requires stamps computed upon the full amount of the contract price, regardless of the date of the contract.

60.07   **Options, contracts of purchase** and **leases** require no stamps. (But see Section 60.12.)

60.08   **Certificates of sale** require stamps, and commissioners' and sheriffs' deeds do not. An **assignment of a certificate of sale** would require stamps if the consideration or value of the interest conveyed exceeded $100.00.
         A **certificate of redemption** from a foreclosure sale has been ruled to be in effect a transfer of the title and therefore subject to the stamp tax.

60.09   In an **exchange** each deed requires stamps, the computation in each case being made on the actual value of the interest or property conveyed, the amount of any pre-existing lien or encumbrance not removed by the sale being deductible.

60.10   **Deeds of release** and **deeds of trust** are not subject to tax.

60.11   Prior to code amendment in 1958, the rule was followed that deed to or by a **state or a political sub-**

division or corporate instrumentality is "not exempt from documentary stamp tax merely by reason of the governmental character of one of the parties of the transaction," under Internal Revenue Department ruling of May 1, 1950 (Bulletin No. 9).

In 1958 the Internal Revenue Code was amended to provide that "No State or Territory or political subdivision thereof, or the District of Columbia, shall be liable for the tax imposed by Section 4361 with respect to any deed, instrument, or writing to which it is a party, and affixing of stamps thereby shall not be deemed payment for the tax, which may be collected by assessment from any other party liable therefor." (26 U.S.C.A. Sec. 4362)

60.12   **Oil and gas leases** of indefinite duration require revenue stamps as conveyances of real property. The commissioner of internal revenue ruled that "in determining the actual value of the lease, consideration should be given to its market value, the value at which it is set up on the books of the grantee or assignee and other surrounding circumstances. If the so-called down payment (bonus) represents a fair consideration for the interest conveyed and not simply a nominal consideration, the tax in such case should be computed on the basis of such consideration."

60.13   The **failure to affix revenue stamps** to a document does not invalidate it or prevent the title passing if it is a deed. In any transaction where it is doubtful whether or not stamps are required, the parties should obtain a ruling from the Internal Revenue Department.

USE TAX
(See Section 11.06F)

USURY

61.01 **USURY LAW**

The subject of usury is covered by the Usury Law of 1918, as modified by constitutional amendment

(Section 22 of Article XX) effective November 6, 1934.

The effect of the amendment was to reduce the maximum permissible interest rate, to exempt certain enumerated classes of lenders from certain provisions of the usury law, and to place in the legislature a certain degree of control over the fixing of charges made by the exempted groups. (**Penziner vs. West American Finance Company,** 10 Cal. (2d) 160.)

61.02 **LEGAL RATE OF INTEREST**

Seven per cent per annum.

61.03 **CONTRACT RATE OF INTEREST**

Parties may contract in writing for a rate of interest not exceeding **10** per cent per annum (with certain exceptions; see paragraph following). Prior to November 6, 1934, the limit was 12 per cent.

61.04 **CORPORATIONS AND PERSONS TO WHOM THE USURY LAW DOES NOT APPLY**

The restrictions of the usury law by the amendment in effect November 6, 1934, do not apply to the following:

Building and loan associations; industrial loan companies; credit unions; pawnbrokers; personal property brokers; banks; non-profit cooperative associations; and corporations, associations, syndicates, joint stock companies or partnerships engaged exclusively in marketing, agricultural, dairy, live stock, poultry and bee products on a cooperative non-profit basis in loaning or advancing money to the members thereof.

Personal property brokers, however, are subject to the provisions of the "Personal Property Brokers Act" and the "California Small Loan Act," as to which see Section 61.07.

61.05 **COMPOUND INTEREST**

Interest cannot be compounded, nor does interest bear interest, unless an agreement to that effect is clearly expressed in writing and signed by the party to be charged.

61.06 EFFECT OF ILLEGAL RATE

No greater rate of interest than 10 per cent per annum can, directly or indirectly, be taken or received for the loan or forbearance of money, goods, or things in action, and any agreement or contract so to do is null and void as to any agreement to pay interest; and no action at law to recover interest in any sum can be maintained, and the debt cannot be declared due until the full period of time it was contracted for has elapsed.

A note which provides for a bonus for the privilege of **prepayment** is not usurious. Provision for any other bonus or commission, however, that results in the maximum permissible interest rate being exceeded, is usurious.

Acceleration of maturity does not result in usury.

61.07

The "Personal Property Brokers Act" and the "California Small Loan Act" restrict the interest and charges that may be made in connection with small loans and bring such lenders under the control of the commissioner of corporations.

VACATION OF STREETS AND HIGHWAYS

62.01 VACATION DOES NOT CHANGE OWNERSHIP OF FEE

The vacation or abandonment of a public highway, street or alley affects only the easement of the public therein. The rights of the public are terminated, but the ownership of the fee is unchanged.

The owners of property adjoining a highway, street or alley are presumed to own to its center (subject to the public easement therein), though the contrary may be shown to be the fact. (See "Descriptions.") Upon vacation or abandonment of the highway, street or alley the adjoining owners continue to hold title to the center (if they already held the fee), but free of the easement of the public.

62.02 **DEED OF LOTS CARRIES VACATED PORTION ADJOINING**

A deed of a lot, by a description that refers to the recorded map of the subdivision that includes the lot, will carry the grantor's title to the center of any adjoining street or alley **shown on the map**—even though the street or alley has been previously vacated, and the deed contains no specific description of the vacated portion. (185 Cal. 386.)

It is the practice of title companies, however, when a deed, mortgage or other instrument is sent in for filing, affecting such lot, to ask that a specific description of the vacated portion be inserted.

A deed of a lot in a tract probably will carry the grantor's title to the center of the vacated street adjoining **if the street was shown on the map,** even though the street was not a part of the tract to which the lot belonged.

62.03 **BOUNDARY STREETS IN A SUBDIVISION**

A deed of a lot adjoining a street that forms the boundary of a subdivision (the street being entirely included within the subdivision) carries the grantor's title at least to the center of the street, and probably to the boundary line of the subdivision.

62.04 **RIGHTS OF ABUTTING AND NON-ABUTTING OWNERS**

Purchasers of lots in a subdivision by reference to a map thereof showing streets acquire private easements in such streets entirely independent of the dedication to public use, and such easements remain after vacation of the public easement for the convenience of the owners in going from each lot to any and all the other lots in the tract so laid off.

Section 812 C.C., effective October 1, 1949 provides that unless persons claiming private easements in vacated streets record notice of such claims in the office of the county recorder within two years from October 1, 1949 or within two years from the effective date of such vacation, all such easements are extinguished, **ex-**

cept a private easement necessary for the purpose of ingress and egress to the lot owned by such person from or to a public street or highway.

62.05 VACATED PROPERTY ADJOINING NON-RECTANGULAR LOTS

Great care should be taken in compiling a description of a vacated strip adjoining a lot, or a portion of a lot, that is not rectangular in shape. There appears to be no legal presumption either that the side lines of such a lot are to be continued directly to the center of the vacated street or alley, or that boundary lines of the vacated portion are to be drawn at right angles to the street or alley lines. A description should be drawn that is logical and acceptable to the party interested, and—if there is any possibility of its encroaching on another's claim—it will be qualified by a title company in its policy, unless deeds are obtained from adjoining claimants.

VENDOR'S LIEN

63.01   The term "vendor's lien," when properly used, refers to the **implied lien,** that is, one not created by mortgage or other express agreement, but given in equity to a vendor of land, who has parted with the title and possession, to secure payment of the unpaid purchase money unsecured otherwise than by the personal obligation of the buyer, as provided by Section 3046 of the Civil Code. (108 Cal. 19.) It is not assignable, although it will pass to the personal representative of a deceased vendor. It may be waived, even without consideration, and is waived by taking any security other than the personal obligation of the buyer. It is valid against everyone claiming under the buyer, except a purchaser or encumbrancer without notice and for value. But it is of no operative force or effect until established by a decree of court in a suit brought for that purpose. The lien may be enforced, unless waived, so long as an action may be commenced for the purchase money. It is based on the equitable doctrine that the grantee should not keep the property without paying for it.

63.02   Such lien is entirely distinct from a lien **expressly reserved** in a deed conveying the property, or in case of the ordinary executory contract for the sale of real property, **where the vendor retains title** as security for the payment of the purchase money, and as trustee for the purchaser, who has only an equitable estate in the land, which becomes absolute upon complying with the contract. Such liens or rights are assignable, and, as incident to the debt, pass with an assignment of the purchase money note or notes. They are not necessarily waived by taking other security. The vendor waives his rights under a contract reserving title until full payment of the purchase money, by executing a conveyance without payment, although he does not thereby waive his vendor's lien implied from the execution of the conveyance. (50 Cal. App. 201.)

ZONING

64.01   Zoning is the public regulation of the use of property. The zoning ordinances of a city regulate, among other things, the use, height and size of buildings and the minimum area of courts and yards. The justification for such ordinances is that they promote public health, safety, comfort, convenience and general welfare.

64.02   Zoning restrictions and private or deed restrictions operate independently of each other. A city cannot abrogate a contract already entered into by two other parties, that is, the seller and the buyer of the lot in question.

LOS ANGELES CITY ZONING

64.03   In Los Angeles, Ordinance No. 90,500 establishes what is called the "Comprehensive Zoning Plan of the City of Los Angeles," which consolidates and coordinates all zoning regulations and provisions into one plan. This ordinance designates, regulates and restricts the location and use of buildings, structures and land, for agriculture, residence, commerce, trade, industry or other purposes. It regulates the height and size of buildings, regulates the open spaces and limits the density of population. As amended to and including Ordinance No. 101,943 it divides the city into 20 zones, these being:

1. "A1" Agricultural Zone
2. "A2" Agricultural Zone
3. "RA" Suburban Zone
4. "RS" Suburban Zone
5. "R1" One-Family Zone
6. "R2" Two-Family Zone
7. "R3" Multiple Dwelling Zone
8. "R4" Multiple Dwelling Zone
9. "R5" Multiple Dwelling Zone
10. "P" Automobile Parking Zone
11. "CR" Limited Commercial Zone
12. "C1" Limited Commercial Zone
13. "C2" Commercial Zone
14. "C3" Commercial Zone
15. "C4" Commercial Zone
16. "C5" Commercial Zone
17. "CM" Commercial Manufacturing Zone
18. "M1" Limited Industrial Zone
19. "M2" Light Industrial Zone
20. "M3" Heavy Industrial Zone

4.04   Where practical difficulties or unnecessary hardships result from the strict and literal interpretation of the provisions of the ordinance, a method is outlined for the obtaining of a **variance** upon submission to the zoning administrator of a verified application from the owner or lessee of the property affected. (This is sometimes called "spot zoning.")

4.05   Provision is also made for the establishment, following the filing of an application by owners or lessee, of **building lines** along any street or portion thereof so as to regulate the distance from the street line at which buildings, structures or improvements may be erected, constructed, established or maintained. (Building lines are sometimes known as "set-back" lines.)

64.06 **CONVEYANCE MADE CONTRARY TO PROVISIONS OF ZONING ORDINANCE**

Section 11540.1, added to the Business and Professions Code on October 1, 1949, provides that any conveyance made contrary to the provisions of an ordinance prescribing the area or dimensions of lots or parcels, or prohibiting the reduction in area or the separation in ownership of land, or requiring the filing of a map of any land to be divided, shall not be invalid. Such ordinance, however, may provide that any deed of conveyance, sale or contract to sell made contrary to its provisions is voidable to the extent and in the same manner as provided in Section 11540 of said Code.

As to any conveyance executed prior to October 1, 1949, and alleged to be in violation of any such municipal or county ordinance or regulation, a proceeding or defense based thereon must be commenced or maintained within one year after the execution of such conveyance or prior to October 1, 1950, whichever time is later.

WORDS, PHRASES
AND
DEFINITIONS

WORDS, PHRASES
AND DEFINITIONS

Ab initio—From the beginning.

Ab initio mundi—From the beginning of the world.

Abstract—An abridgment; as applied to a record, it means a complete history in short, abbreviated form; a summary.

Abstract of judgment—A brief transcript of the essentials of a judgment.

Abstract of title—A summary or epitome of the conveyances, transfers and other facts relied on as evidence of title, together with all such facts appearing of record as may impair the title.

Abutting owners—Those owners whose lands touch a highway or other public place.

Acceleration Clause—Clause in a deed of trust or mortgage which "accelerates"—that is, hastens—the time when the indebtedness becomes due; for example, some deeds of trust contain a provision (an acceleration clause) that the note shall become due immediately upon the sale of the land or upon failure to pay interest or an installment of principal and interest.

Accommodation—An obligation assumed without consideration.

Accretion—(See topic of "Accretion.")

Action for separate maintenance—An action by a married woman who is compelled through her husband's fault to live apart from him, by which action she is allowed separate maintenance or permanent alimony without divorce.

Action in personam—An action which has for its object a judgment against the person as distinguished from a judgment against property to determine its status. (Example: an action for services rendered.)

Action in rem—An action which has for its object a judgment against property to determine its status. (Example: an action to foreclose a mortgage.)

Action to quiet title—An action to effect the removal of a cloud or clouds on title to property.

Act of God—Any irresistible disaster, the result of natural causes, such as earthquakes, violent storms, lightning, unprecedented floods.

Ad—At; to; before; near; for; of; until; within.

Ad curiam—Before the court; to the court.

Ad litem—During the pendency of the action or proceeding.

Administrator—A person appointed by a probate court to settle the estate of a person who died and left no will.

Administrator C.T.A.—Abbreviation for administrator cum testamento annexo.

Administrator cum testamento annexo—An administrator with the will annexed, that is, an administrator of a decedent whose will named no executor or named an executor who can not or will not act.

Administrator D.B.N.—Abbreviation for administrator de bonis non—"de bonis non" meaning: of goods or property upon which no administration has been had.

Administrator de bonis non—See above.

Ad valorem—According to value.

Adverse possession—The open and notorious possession and occupation of real property under an evident claim or color of right.

Affiant—A person who has made an affidavit.

Agenda—Things to be done; matters to be attended to.

Alcalde—Chief magistrate or mayor. (Spanish.)

Alias—Also known as. (Shortened from **alias dictus**, "otherwise called.")

Alienate—To transfer property to another; to alien.

Alimony—An allowance to either spouse upon a decree of divorce or pending the suit (pendente lite).

Aliter—Otherwise.

Allegation—An assertion; a statement of fact in a pleading.

Alluvion—The soil deposited by accretion.

Ancillary—Auxiliary.

Ante—Before.

Antenuptial—Before marriage.

Appearance—The coming into court of a party to a suit.

Appurtenant—That which belongs to another thing, but which has not belonged to it immemorially.

A priori—From the past; from what has previously transpired.

Arbitrary map—An office "subdivision" or map made by a title company for its own convenience in locating property in an area in which all the descriptions are by metes and bounds. On this "subdivision," the "lots" are given "arbitrary" numbers. The deeds and other instruments affecting these "lots" are posted to what is called an "arbitrary" account. The word "arbitrary" is often shortened to "arb."

Assumpsit—An undertaking, express or implied, to do some act or make some payment.

Attestation clause—That clause in a deed denoting that the persons signing are witnesses.

Attorn—To accept and acknowledge a new landlord; to appoint an attorney or substitute.

Avulsion—The sudden and perceptible tearing away or separation of land by the violent action of contiguous water.

Ayuntamiento—Town council. (Spanish.)

Benevolent associations—Voluntary aggregations of individuals or bodies corporate formed, not for profit, but to render financial aid or other assistance to members.

Bequest—A testamentary gift of personal property. The term has sometimes been held to include real property also.

Betterment—Substantial improvements upon real property. (More than mere repairs.)

b.f.—Abbreviation of "bonum factum," meaning a good deed. A valid decree.

Bid—An offer (noun).

Bill of Sale—A written instrument evidencing the transfer of title to personal property from seller to purchaser.

Blue Sky Laws—Statutes regulating investment companies, the conduct of their business and the issuance and sale of their securities.

Bona—Goods; chattels.

Bonae fidei emptor—A purchaser in good faith.

Bona fide—In good faith; without fraud.

Bonded debt—An indebtedness secured by a bond issue.

Bounds—Boundaries.

Building line—Lines established by ordinance or statute between which and the street the property owner may not build.

By-law—A rule of a corporation for its government.

Camino—A highway. (Spanish.)

Capita—Heads; persons.

Capitation taxes—Poll taxes.

Caption—The heading or title of a document.

Cause—An action or suit.

Caveat—Let him beware. A formal warning against the performance of certain acts.

Caveat emptor—Let the buyer beware, that is, when the parties are on an equal footing, the buyer must examine the goods and make the purchase at his own peril.

C.C.; C.C.P.—Civil Code; Code of Civil Procedure.

Certiorari—A writ from a superior to an inferior court, directing a certified record of its proceedings in a designated case to be sent up for review.

Cestui—He.

Cestui que trust—The person for whose benefit property is held in trust by a trustee.

Cestui que use—The person for whose use land was granted to another.

Cestui que vie—The person for the duration of whose lifetime an estate has been granted.

Change of venue—The removal of a cause for trial from one county to another.

Chattels—Personal property; any estate less than a freehold.

Chose in action—A thing in action, that is, a thing of which the owner has not possession but only a right to bring an action for its possession or for damages.

Circa—About; around; concerning.

Code—A system of law.

Collateral—Indirect; blood relationship other than lineal.

Color of title—That which gives the appearance of title, but is not title in fact.

Common Law—(a) The body of customs, usages and practices developed and administered by the Anglo-Saxons. The body of English Law as distinguished from Roman Law, canon law, and other systems.

(b) The ancient unwritten law founded on immemorial customs and precedents as distinguished from statute law.

Communis paries—a party wall.

Competent—Legally qualified; possessing adequate mental capacity.

Composition—An agreement between a debtor and his creditors whereby the latter mutually agree to accept a certain percentage less than is due each one.

Condemnation—The exercise of the power of eminent domain; that is, the taking of private property for public use.

Conditional sale contract—A contract for the sale of goods, the goods to be delivered to the buyer, the seller to retain, however, title thereof until the conditions of the contract have been fulfilled.

Condominium—Ownership of a divided interest, i.e., an individually owned unit, in a multi-family or other structure.

Confession of judgment—An entry of judgment upon the admission or confession of the debtor without the formality, time or expense involved in an ordinary proceeding.

Congressional grant—A grant of public land of the United States made by an act of Congress.

Conservator—A person appointed to take care of the property of an adult person who by reason of advanced age, illness, or other cause is unable to properly care for his property.

Consideration—The inducement which moves a party to enter into a contract.

Constructive notice—Notice given by the public records. Generally, the law presumes that one has the same knowledge of instruments properly recorded as if he were actually acquainted with them.

Contiguous—In actual or close contact; touching; adjacent; near.

Contingent—Dependent upon an uncertain future event.

Corp. C.—Corporations Code.

Corporal—Affecting or relating to the body.

Corporation—An artificial being created by law and endowed with certain of the rights, privileges and duties of natural persons.

Corporation sole—A corporation consisting of a single person, and his successor, incorporated by law to give such person certain advantages, particularly that of perpetuity, which otherwise he could not have had. (An example is The Roman Catholic Archbishop of Los Angeles.)

Corporeal—Having a body; tangible.

Corporeal hereditaments—Such inheritable property as may be perceived by the senses.

Croft—A small farm.

c. t. a.—An abbreviation of **cum testamento annexo.** (With will annexed.) See **Administrator C.T.A.**

Curtesy—The life estate or the tenure which (in some states, but not in California) the husband has in the lands of his deceased wife, which by the common law takes effect where he has had issue by her, born alive, and capable of inheriting the lands.

d. b. n.—An abbreviation of de bonis non. (See **Administrator D.B.N.**)

d. d.—An abbreviation of "days after date."

De—From; of; concerning.

Deed—Written document by which the ownership of land is transferred from one person to another.

Deed of trust—Written document by which the title to the land is conveyed as security for the repayment of a loan.

De facto—In fact.

Deficiency judgment—A personal judgment against any person liable for the mortgage or trust deed debt for the amount remaining due the mortgagee or beneficiary after foreclosure.

Defunct—Dead.

De jure—By right.

Demise—A transfer; a lease; a transfer to another of an estate for years, for life or at will.

Deponent—A witness; an affiant.

Deraign—To trace; to prove.

Descent—Transmission of an estate by inheritance.

Devise—A gift of real property by will.

Devisee—A person to whom real property is given by will.

Dicta—Plural of dictum.

Dictum—An opinion by a judge on a point not essential to the decision on the main question.

Dies—A day.

Diluvion—The gradual washing away and consequent loss of soil along the banks of a river.

Disseisin—Ouster.

Divest—To deprive of a right or title.

Divisa—A boundary.

Dona—Gifts.

Donee—A person to whom a gift is made.

Donor—A person who makes a gift.

Dower—The legal right or interest which the wife acquires (in some states but not in California) by marriage in the real estate of her husband.

D.S.—Declaratory statement. (Abbreviation used in Land Office.)

Earnest—Something given as a part of the purchase price to bind a bargain.

Easement—A right or interest in the land of another which entitles the holder thereof to some use, privilege, or benefit (such as to place pole lines, pipe lines, roads thereon, or travel over, etc.) out of or over said land.

Eleemosynary—Charitable.

Elisor—A person appointed to perform certain duties pertaining to certain officers (especially sheriff or coroner) when the latter are disqualified.

Eminent domain—The right or power of the government to take private property for public use on making just compensation therefor.

Emptor—A buyer.

Enfeoff—To vest a person with the fee.

Entirety—A tenancy in which the parties are jointly seized of the whole.

Equitable title—The right in the party to whom it belongs to have the legal title transferred to him.

Equity of redemption—The right which the mortgagor of an estate has of redeeming it, after it has been forfeited at law by the non-payment of the money it was given to secure.

Erosion—The gradual eating away of the soil by the operation of currents or tides.

Escheat—The lapsing or reverting of land to the state.

Escrow—A transaction in which a third party acts as the agent for seller and buyer, or for borrower and lender, in carrying out the instructions of both and handling and disbursing the papers and funds.

Estoppel—A bar which precludes a person, in law, from asserting rights in contravention of his previous position or representations.

Et al.—And others. (From the Latin **et alii**.)

Executor—A man appointed by a testator to carry out the provisions of his will.

Executrix—A woman appointed as above.

Expediente—Early California (Spanish and Mexican) land grant file. A complete statement of every step taken in the proceedings to acquire a Spanish or Mexican grant.

Ex post facto—After the event.

Express—Definite; clear.

Facsimile—An exact and precise copy.

Facta—Facts; deeds; acts.

Fee—An estate of inheritance in land.

Fee simple—An absolute fee; a fee without limitation to any particular class of heirs or restrictions.

Feme covert—A married woman.

Feme sole—An unmarried woman.

Fiduciary—Held or founded in trust.

Freehold—An estate of inheritance, an estate for life or an estate during the life of a third person.

Garnish—To cause a garnishment to be levied on a person.

Garnishment—A proceeding whereby property, money or credits of a debtor in possession of another (the garnishee) are applied to the payment of the debts by means of process against the debtor and garnishee.

Gore—A small, triangular piece of land.

Gov't. C.—Government Code.

Groin—Any structure offering or intended to offer substantial resistance to the coastwise movement of littoral sands.

Guardian—A person to whom the law has entrusted the custody and control of the person or estate, or both, of a minor or incompetent person.

Habendum—That clause in a deed (not required in California) which recites "to have and to hold to said grantee(s), his (her or their) heirs, successors and assigns (as separate property—joint tenants—tenants in common)."

Habendum et tenendum—To have and to hold.

Hand—A lineal measure of four inches.

Heirs—Those who are entitled by law to inherit the property of a deceased person.

Hereditaments—Anything capable of being inherited.

Holographic will—A will entirely written, dated and signed by the testator in his own handwriting.

Hypothecate—To give a thing as security without parting with the possession thereof.

Idem sonans—The doctrine that if two names may be sounded alike any variance in spelling is immaterial and the names are **idem sonans.**

Id est—That is; that is to say.

i.e.—An abbreviation of id est.

In esse—In being; alive.

In personam—Against the person.

In propria persona—In his own person; himself; as, the defendant appears **in propria persona.**

In re—In the matter of.

In rem—Against a thing and not against a person.

Inter alia—Among other things.

Interlocutory decree—A decree made pending the final outcome of the cause and before a final hearing on the merits of the case.

Intestate—Without a will; a person who has died without leaving a will.

Intra—Within.

Inure—To serve to the use or benefit.

Ipso facto—Of itself; by the very fact.

Joinder—Acting jointly with one or more persons; joining.

Jurat—A certificate evidencing the fact that an affidavit was properly made before a duly authorized officer.

Jurisdiction—The right to adjudicate concerning the subject matter in a given case.

Labor—A measure of land in Mexico and Texas equal to 177½ acres.

Laches—Inexcusable delay in asserting a right.

Landowner's royalty—That interest in unsevered oil and gas which is retained or reserved to the landowner on the occasion of his alienation of an interest in the real property involved.

Latent—Concealed.

Lateral—Pertaining to, proceeding from, or directed toward the side.

Lease—Written document by which the possession of land or a building is given by the owner to another person for a specified period of time and for the rent specified.

Legatee—One to whom personal property is bequeathed in a will.

Lien—A charge upon property for the payment or discharge of a debt or duty.

Lineal—In a direct line.

Lis pendens—Suit pending; notice of action.

Lite pendente—While the action is pending.

Littoral—Pertaining to the shore.

Marketability—The status of a title, when viewed in the light of whether or not it is in such a condition as to attract a purchaser.

Mean—Intermediate.

Meander—To follow a winding course.

Memorial—A short note, abstract or memorandum.

Mesne—Intermediate; intervening; mean.

Metes and Bounds—Measurements and boundaries.

Moratorium—The temporary suspension by statute of the enforcement of liability for debt.

Mortgage—A written document by which land is put up as security for the repayment of a loan.

Muniments of title—Title deeds and other original documents showing a chain of title.

Naturalization—The grant of citizenship to an alien by the nation.

Naturalized citizen—A person who has been made a citizen of the United States under an act of Congress.

Neap tides—Those tides which happen between the full and change of the moon, twice in every twenty-four hours.

Non sequitur—It does not follow.

Nonsuit—A judgment given against the plaintiff when he is unable to prove a case or when he refuses or neglects to proceed to the trial after it has been put at issue without determining such issue.

Novation—The substitution of a new obligation in place of an existing one.

Nulla bona return—The return of the sheriff or other officer on execution unsatisfied. (Nulla bona means "no goods.")

Nunc pro tunc—Now for then. A tardy act made retroactive so as to take effect as of the time when it should have been done.

Nuncupative will—A will declared orally and not in writing.

Obiter dictum—That which is said in passing.

Obiter dicta—Plural of obiter dictum.

Omnibus clause—That clause in a decree of distribution by which "any other property not now known or discovered which may belong to said estate or in which said estate may have any interest" passes to the distributees named without specific description.

Operative property—Any property which may be reasonably necessary for use in the operation and conduct of the particular kind or kinds of business in which such property is employed.

Option—A right, for a consideration, to do or require an act to be done in the future; choice.

Oral—Verbal; spoken.

Overriding royalty—That interest in unsevered oil and gas which the lessee retains on the occasion of his executing a sublease or assignment.

Overt—Open.

Pol. C.—Political Code.

Pari passu—In equal degree; pro rata.

Parol—Oral.

Participating per cent—Any interest in the unsevered oil and gas which the owner, lessee, sublessee, or assignee disposes of to investors to finance directly or indirectly the business enterprise whereby the purchaser, assignee, or investor is to share proportionately in the income from such an enterprise conducted by others.

Party wall—A wall for the common benefit and use of two owners, their property being separated by the wall.

Patent—A conveyance of title to government land by the government.

Pendente lite—Pending suit.

Per autre vie—During the life of another.

Per capita—By the head, that is, by the number of individuals.

Per se—By itself; as such.

Per stirpes—According to the roots; by right of representation.

Pleadings—The successive statements by which the plaintiff sets forth his cause and claim, and the defendant his defense.

Pledge—A pawn; a bailment of personal property as security for some debt or engagement.

Post—After; afterward. (Adverb.)

Preamble—An introductory portion.

Pre-emption—The act of buying anything before or ahead of another person.

Pre-emption entry—An entry by a settler upon public lands of the United States in connection with which the entryman secures a preferred right to acquire the land by virtue of his occupation and improvement.

Prescription—Title obtained in law by long possession. Occupancy for the period prescribed by the Code of Civil Procedure as sufficient to bar an action for the recovery of the property gives title by prescription.

Pretermit—To omit; to pass by.

Prima facie—On its face; presumptively.

Privity—Closeness or mutuality of relationship.

Prob. C.—Probate Code.

Pro tanto—For so much; to that extent.

Publ. Res. C.—Public Resources Code.

Quasi—As; as if; of a similar nature.

q.v.—(Quod vide.) Which see.

Ratable—Proportionate.

Reddendum—A reservation in a deed whereby the grantor reserves some new thing to himself out of that which he has granted.

Redemption—The buying back of one's property after it has been sold.

Reliction—Gradual recession of water from the usual water-mark.

Remainder—The estate limited by the grantor to take effect in a third person upon the termination of a preceding estate.

Remittitur—The term employed to designate the judgment of the appellate tribunal which is authenticated to the court from which the appeal is taken or over which its controlling jurisdiction is exercised.

Residuary legatee—One who receives the residue of an estate after the payment of the testator's debt and legacies.

Residuum—Balance, residue.

Riparian—Pertaining to the bank of a river.

Sans—Without.

Scilicet—To wit; that is to say; namely. Abbreviated as **ss** (used in acknowledgments).

Seisin—⎰The possession of land under a claim of a freehold.
Seizin—⎱That which is possessed. The act of taking possession.

Seriatim—In succession.

Situs—Location.

ss—Abbreviation of **scilicet**, which see.

Stare decisis—The doctrine that the decisions of court should stand as precedents for future guidance. (Let that which has been decided stand.)

Stirps—(plural, **stirpes**)—Stock, race, family. Hence, in law, the person from whom a family is descended. (See **Per stirpes.**)

Subordinate—To make subject.

Subrogate—To substitute one person in the place of another with reference to a claim or right.

Testament—The written declaration of one's last will.

Testamonium clause—The concluding clause of an instrument, beginning, "In witness whereof."

Toll—(verb)—To bar; to defeat.

Toll the statute—To stop the running of the statute of limitations, as on a debt, by making a new promise to pay.

Tort—Wrong; a civil wrong not arising out of a contract.

Trust deed—See Deed of Trust.

Ultra vires—Beyond their powers. A corporation is said to act "ultra vires" when it exceeds the authority imparted to it.

Vendee—Purchaser.

Vendor—Seller.

Venue—Neighborhood; the county in which a suit is brought, or the place in which an acknowledgment is taken.

Versus—Against. (Abbreviated vs. or v.)

Vide—See.

Videlicet—To-wit; that is to say.

Viz.—Videlicet; namely.

Waiver—Act of waiving or intentionally relinquishing or abandoning some known right, claim or privilege.

Warrant—To guarantee.

INDEX

INDEX

(For terms not listed hereunder, see "Words, Phrases and Definitions.")

OFFICES OF TITLE INSURANCE AND TRUST COMPANY

AND ITS AFFILIATE COMPANIES IN CALIFORNIA

ALAMEDA COUNTY · GLencourt 1-8300
Title Insurance and Trust Company
1459 Franklin Street, Oakland 12

BUTTE COUNTY · FIreside 2-8323
*Mid-Valley Title and Escrow Company
183 East Sixth Street, Chico

CALAVERAS COUNTY · SKyline 4-3533
*Northern California Title Company
P. O. Box 806, San Andreas

CONTRA COSTA COUNTY · ACademy 8-2400
Title Insurance and Trust Company
Main & Court Streets, Martinez

EL DORADO COUNTY · NAtional 2-3135
*Inter-County Title Company
451 Main Street, Placerville

FRESNO COUNTY · ADams 3-7731
Title Insurance and Trust Company
1246 "L" Street, Fresno 21

GLENN COUNTY · WEllington 4-4557
*Estate Title and Abstract Company, Inc.
115 South Butte Street, Willows

IMPERIAL COUNTY · ELgin 2-4661
Title Insurance and Trust Company
600 Main Street, El Centro

INYO COUNTY · INdependence 2-011
Title Insurance and Trust Company
224 North Edwards Street, Independence

KERN COUNTY · FAirview 7-7311
Title Insurance and Trust Company
1715 Chester Ave., Bakersfield

KINGS COUNTY · LUdlow 2-0344
*Hanford Title Company
318 North Irwin Street, Hanford

LOS ANGELES COUNTY · 626-2411
Title Insurance and Trust Company
433 S. Spring St., Los Angeles 54

MARIN COUNTY · GLenwood 4-4273
Title Insurance and Trust Company
1200 Lincoln Ave., San Rafael

MERCED COUNTY · 722-3586
Title Insurance and Trust Company
525 W. 20th Street, Merced

MONO COUNTY · INdependence 2-011
Title Insurance and Trust Company
224 North Edwards Street, Independence

MONTEREY COUNTY · HArrison 4-8011
Title Insurance and Trust Company
16 W. Gabilan St., Salinas

NAPA COUNTY · BAldwin 4-7803
*California Pacific Title Company
950 Randolph St., Napa

NEVADA COUNTY · 71
*Inter-County Title Company
231 Commercial St., Nevada City

ORANGE COUNTY · 547-3333
Title Insurance and Trust Company
800 North Main St., Santa Ana

PLACER COUNTY · TUrner 5-6251
Title Insurance and Trust Company
110 Maple St., Auburn

RIVERSIDE COUNTY · OVerland 6-4180
Title Insurance and Trust Company
3490 Tenth St., Riverside

SACRAMENTO COUNTY · HIckory 4-8300
Title Insurance and Trust Company
2101 "K" St., Sacramento

SAN BERNARDINO COUNTY · TUrner 9-3511
Title Insurance and Trust Company
340 Fourth St., San Bernardino

SAN DIEGO COUNTY · 239-6081
Title Insurance and Trust Company
220 "A" St., San Diego

SAN FRANCISCO COUNTY · SUtter 1-3500
Title Insurance and Trust Company
148 Montgomery St., San Francisco 4

SAN JOAQUIN COUNTY · HOward 6-0121
Title Insurance and Trust Company
345 North El Dorado St., Stockton

SAN LUIS OBISPO COUNTY · LIberty 3-2900
Title Insurance and Trust Company
1141 Chorro St., San Luis Obispo

SAN MATEO COUNTY · EMerson 6-9551
Title Insurance and Trust Company
333 Marshall, Redwood City

SANTA BARBARA COUNTY · WOodland 5-0571
Title Insurance and Trust Company
36 E. Figueroa St., Santa Barbara

SANTA CLARA COUNTY · CYpress 2-4212
Title Insurance and Trust Company
66 North First St., San Jose 13

SANTA CRUZ COUNTY · GArden 3-5272
Title Insurance and Trust Company
Front at Cooper Sts., Santa Cruz

SHASTA COUNTY · CHestnut 3-4525
*North Valley Title & Escrow Company
1600 West St., Redding

SONOMA COUNTY · LIberty 6-1195
Title Insurance and Trust Company
538 Mendocino Ave., Santa Rosa

STANISLAUS COUNTY · LAmbert 9-0521
Title Insurance and Trust Company
1207 Eye St., Modesto

TEHAMA COUNTY · LAurence 7-5421
*Northern California Title Company
349 Pine St., Red Bluff

TULARE COUNTY · REdwood 2-2271
Title Insurance and Trust Company
320 W. Main St., Visalia

VENTURA COUNTY · MIller 3-2275
Title Insurance and Trust Company
101 S. Chestnut St., Ventura

*Affiliated by Underwriting Agreements